MW00639876

Jesus:

An Obedient Son

Jesus:

An Obedient Son

MICHAEL PHILLIPS

Destiny Image® Publishers, Inc.
P.O. Box 310
Shippensburg, PA 17257-0310

"Speaking to the Purposes of God for This Generation
and for the Generations to Come"

ISBN 0-7684-2070-9

For Worldwide Distribution
Printed in the U.S.A.

This book and all other Destiny Image, Revival Press,
MercyPlace, Fresh Bread, Destiny Image Fiction,
and Treasure House books are available
at Christian bookstores and distributors worldwide.

For a U.S. bookstore nearest you, call **1-800-722-6774**.
For more information on foreign distributors, call **717-532-3040**.
Or reach us on the Internet:
www.destinyimage.com

THE BOND OF THE UNIVERSE, THE CHAIN
THAT HOLDS IT TOGETHER, THE ONE ACTIVE
UNITY, THE HARMONY OF THINGS, IS THE
DEVOTION OF THE SON TO THE FATHER.
IT IS THE LIFE OF THE UNIVERSE.
—GEORGE MACDONALD

Contents

Introduction

The Man on Everyone's Mind

No name is so familiar to so many as the name *Jesus Christ.*
Familiar...yes. Understood, no.

Two words...known but unknown, enigmatic, mysterious. Few men and women know very much about the man Jesus who walked this earth almost exactly two thousand years ago.

Most know scattered facts about Him. Details chronicled by His biographers, overlaid by traditions and religious teaching passed down through time.

But the *why* that brought Him among us sadly remains veiled.

That is not to say we haven't tried to know Him.

His brief walk across the pages of time reverberated with such force that it might be likened to the Big Bang of human history. Nothing literally since the foundation of the universe itself set off such titanic explosions of change. And the effects have not stopped in twenty centuries.

Yet when the brief 33 years of His life are examined at a glance, one finds no explanation for such global and permanent repercussions. On the surface of it, the evidence reveals little more than an itinerant carpenter-preacher from an obscure village in a remote and insignificant corner of the world. Nothing about His subsequent impact makes sense from His biography when interpreted through human eyes. He did not travel. He was not highly educated. He did not write. He was not a political force.

He mounted no coup. He had no army of followers. In fact, He conspicuously did what He could to prevent a mass movement from building up around Him. His teaching was neither complicated nor inflammatory. In large measure the message that drew people to Him could be summed up in the words, "Love God and be nice to those around you." In the end He was executed as a common criminal.

Where in that is the power to shift all history? What can account for it?

These many *whys* ultimately reduce to the simpler, but perhaps more probing question of *who*. Who was this remarkable being who influenced an entire planet? Because once He walked out of the grave, the question of *Who?* suddenly overshadowed all the facts of His prior biography?

For two thousand years most people haven't quite been able to figure out the answer. But the whole world is intrigued. Was He really...*God?*

Everywhere one turns this fascination is evident. Whether believers or not, people are drawn to Jesus by a magnetic pull unlike what they feel from anyone else.

In an offering for a secular book club I was perusing only moments ago, ten of the books listed out of a hundred or so, directly or indirectly concerned the man Jesus Christ and His unprecedented impact on history. No other figure was so prominent.

This Christ-curiosity is almost a passion in the Western world, though largely an invisible one. We tend to categorize the obsessions of modern Western culture under such headings as money, sex, entertainment, leisure, and so on. However, I am convinced that an unseen, silent fascination with Jesus Christ also ranks right up near the top, in the secular world as well as the spiritual. It lurks below the surface, influencing people in ways they never dream of.

Jesus is on everyone's mind.

When a man slams a hammer onto his thumb with full force...when anger rears its head and suddenly a shout of profanity bursts from the lips...when an exclamation of shock or surprise is registered by an unthinking epithet...when careless tongues bandy about a name to punctuate speech for emphasis or deprecation...

To whom does the world turn with its curses, loose talk, and oaths?

Such invectives are not usually shouted out with the words, "Adolf Hitler!" or, "Julius Caesar!"

One never hears the names Napoléon, Buddha, or Genghis Khan used for no reason in the midst of low and debasing speech.

As a boy I recall hearing an irritable bus driver swear at my mother for being a little slow getting three tired children onto his bus when we were trying to find our way through San Francisco late one night. But his words were not, "Alexander the Great, lady...hurry up!"

When at the end of life's rope, with no place to turn, when despair is total and everything seems hopeless, do people sink to their knees in the despondency of aloneness, and whisper, "Martin Luther...please help me!"

In all these situations and circumstances that we observe about us every day, it is *Jesus* who is on the tongues and in the hearts of the world's men and women. It is *Jesus* to whom the lonely and disconsolate cry. It is *Jesus* whose name one hears everywhere, from locker rooms to board-rooms. It is *Jesus* who is as likely to appear on the cover of *Time* as the magazine's Person of the Year.

Why?

One might say that such responses are mere habit, that they reveal nothing of significance. But I think there is more to it than that. Why is *Jesus* the focal point of such habits rather than Muhammad, Gandhi, or George Washington?

Something deeper is going on.

Why is Jesus, even if subconsciously, on the minds of bus drivers, high school students, priests, senior citizens, pastors, Christians, Jews, Muslims, atheists, the editors of magazines?

Even those who might not believe He ever lived at all, or who care nothing about Him...Jesus is on their minds too.

He is the man on *everyone's* mind.

As a result, more has been written about Him than any other human being who has ever lived. But as curious as we are, the multitude of books and articles—thousands, perhaps hundreds of thousands—has in fact accomplished little to reveal Him.

The meaning of His life remains a mystery to many.

What, then, can unlock the mystery of that solitary life lived so long ago in ancient Palestine?

One of the most important factors enabling me to do so is simply this: I try to read the gospel account as an *eyewitness*...as if I am actually there and am caught up in the drama myself.

Sometimes we have to go back to the book and read it afresh, as if encountering the man Jesus for the very first time.

I would like to propose, then, that you and I do just that here together. Can we shake free from our preconceptions and read the gospel as if we have never heard it before, as if suddenly Jesus appeared in our day, in our time, in the midst of our lives, saying and doing extraordinary things?

I propose that we find a way to get inside the account, to get past the "text," past our familiarity with various passages and parables and teachings...past the historical document.

It isn't even enough to try to read the story "as if" we are there. I hope we can find a way to actually be there.

In other words...to put ourselves into the story, and to bring that story alive right now in the midst of our contemporary lives.

I propose that we read the gospel as modern-day eyewitnesses. Can we, in fact, not merely "read" the startling words that fell from the lips of Jesus, but can we actually hear them by our own participation in the incredible drama that turned the world upside down?

Can we experience the immediacy of that impact as He walked along the seashore of Galilee, through the countryside of Judea, into the fateful streets of Jerusalem...and ultimately forward through history into the present-day world where we live right now?

If we can do so, the name Jesus Christ will never be the same again.

Michael Phillips
Eureka, California

PART 1

Jesus Lives Now

One

A Real Man

WHEREVER YOU AND I FIND OURSELVES at this moment, we share something in common in connection with the man Jesus Christ.

We have come together to learn more of Him. Before we even begin, however, we can immediately discover one fact that will be true for both of us. And it is an important fact.

We don't embark on this journey with a clean slate.

Our brains are already full of ideas about Jesus—preconceptions and images. Every one of us, whether we've thought about it or not, possess a series of mental pictures embedded in our consciousness—from His physical features to what He wore, from how He spoke to the crowds to the circumstances and setting of the crucifixion.

Mostly we are all full of *ideas* about Jesus, beliefs and opinions, some no doubt accurate and some inaccurate—things we've been taught, things we've read or heard, maybe conclusions we've drawn on our own.

Whether you consider yourself one of His followers or not, whether you are a pastor, a priest, a layman, a man, a woman, a child, you cannot escape this fact. Neither can I. We're full of impressions that color and distort the way we respond to everything we hear about Jesus. They influence how we hear and receive the words He spoke. At the mention of His name, a dozen mental pictures and opinions concerning this or that, all rise in your brain no less than they do mine.

To undertake an exploration in any field of endeavor requires a recognition of where one happens to be at the outset. And with respect to an inquiry about Jesus, this is where you and I find ourselves. We have to recognize that we are not in the position of a jungle native of the 19th century listening to the Christian missionary speak of Jesus, who, hearing His name for the first time, looks up with puzzled expression and says, "Who? I have never heard of this person."

These preconceptions we bring to this discussion are a huge stumbling block. They obscure our capacity to probe the gospel account in a way that unlocks fresh understanding. Our mental slates are already too full.

Increasing this hindrance, the pages of the gospel on which the story is presented, by their very appearance, *look* like a "religious" document. They do not contain the same power to draw us into their drama with big eyes and pumping hearts and senses fully awake as does a wide-screen THX Hollywood thriller. The double columns and footnotes and marginal references on the page of almost any Bible you pick up look stale and dry and impersonal, as a text to be studied, not a drama to be lived.

And if we're reading the account in 17th-century King James English, the barriers to intimacy become insurmountable. How can we possibly get "into" the story if people are calling each other *thee* and *thou* and using words like *wouldest* and *doth* and *verily* and *brethren*. We've never heard people talk like that in our lives.

We are used to personal...real...gripping...intimate...edge of your seat stuff. But we don't find it in a double-column, footnoted, *ye, hath*, and *shouldest* account.

So how can we put ourselves into the drama...and how can we make it live?

How can we rip up the top sheet of our mental slates to clear them of our preconceptions and images? How can we approach the gospel account fresh, as if we've never heard it before...as if we are really *there*?

Let's turn that question around. Perhaps the imperative upon us is not so much to put ourselves into the gospel world, but to bring the gospel into our world. To read it, not as if we were there, but as if the gospel story suddenly exploded to life *here*...to read as if somehow we were being drawn right into the center of it.

4

We have to realize what it was like for Peter, James, John, Andrew, Mary, Martha, Lazarus, Mary Magdalene, and all the rest of the people who found themselves swept into the story we are so familiar with. They were just going about in the midst of very ordinary lives, when suddenly the Big Bang of history swept them up into it like a human tornado.

To those unsuspecting residents of Capernaum and Magdala and Cana and other small towns throughout Galilee, the name "Jesus" was like any other common name of the day. In their ears it sounded like Bob, Harry, Jess, or Ralph would to us. When they first made His acquaintance, it wasn't an occurrence of epic proportions, as if one day a man in a white robe walked up to you or me and said in solemn tones to the accompaniment of thunder in the sky, "My name is JE...SUS..."

We would be stunned. Such an event would leave us speechless and with mouth gaping open.

But for the people of His day, though their mouths would hang open in astonishment soon enough, at first it wasn't like that at all. They had no clue who he was. To get a feel for the reality of it, imagine the following:

"Hello, Peter, my name is Jess. I'm a carpenter from over in Centerville."

"Hey, how's it going, Jess? Call me Pete."

"How's the fishing today?"

"Not so good."

"Interested in catching something better than just fish?"

"Uh...I'm not sure what you mean."

"Then come with me and I'll tell you about it."

It was down-to-earth stuff. Real.

Now please don't get me wrong. They knew *something* was unique about this extraordinary Nazarene right from the beginning. Nothing else can explain the sudden impact throughout Galilee the moment He burst on the scene.

But they didn't know what that uniqueness was. Because in the midst of that uniqueness, He was a human being just like them.

He felt things, He got hungry, He had to eat, His hair got dirty, His feet got dusty, He sweat and smelled just like any other person, He had to go to the bathroom.

5

Jesus didn't float along six inches off the ground. He was a *man*. He lived life as we must live it. That very manhood is what made it so difficult for those closest to Him to figure out who He really was.

Does such talk make you squirm a bit, as if I am de-spiritualizing the sanctity of our Lord's life?

We have to de-spiritualize it somewhat in order to understand what really went on, and to grasp the enormous spiritual significance of a seemingly ordinary man suddenly working miracles and calling Himself the Christ. I don't think one is ready to lay hold of the import of Jesus's life and character until He can place side by side in His brain two startling facts: If He didn't wash them, Jesus's feet smelled...and He was the Son of God.

We cannot begin to comprehend the magnificence of the incarnation until we apprehend the reality of Jesus's manhood.

So the people surrounding Jesus in the gospel story were no different from you and me. They were just men and women like the rest of us.

They were, however, different in this way. They weren't *taught* about Jesus. They didn't find out about Him from a leather-bound, double-column edition of papyrus scroll they bought from the synagogue bookstore. They found out about Him because all of a sudden there He was in their midst, a compelling man whose words were like nothing they'd ever heard, and who was Himself like no other person who had ever lived.

Unlike us, they *were* like the native asking, "Who?"

As much as possible, then, we've got to put ourselves in their sandals.

Two

Putting Ourselves
in the Story

CLEARING THE PRECONCEPTIONS FROM OUR MENTAL SLATES is not as easy as it might seem.

As much as it may appear that we are no longer a "Christian" culture, we cannot help being inundated all our lives with subtle impressions about Jesus, both from within the Church and outside it. These make it extremely difficult to feel the *newness* of the gospel as it burst upon the world of Galilee and Judea two thousand years ago.

Now we can envision the world of Roman-occupied Palestine of that era. We can try to *imagine* what it was like when a man appeared who began to do things like turn water into wine, calm storms, walk on water, heal people, drive out demons, and draw large crowds and talk about God differently than any Jewish rabbi or prophet ever had. And that is helpful, trying to immerse oneself in that ancient world.

But I find it difficult to put myself into that picture. It's not that I am incapable of conjuring up mental visions. But they are distant, far removed from the here and now of my daily existence. They are images from movies like *Ben Hur*, *The Robe*, and *The Big Fisherman*, from television documentaries and miniseries, from books I have read, and from my study of the New Testament.

But it is not *my* world.

I'm not part of a culture where people wear robes, where Roman legions ride about on horseback, where a nomadic lifestyle is still prevalent, where sheep and goats are likely to fill the streets of a city, where people sleep on the floor and travel by foot and sacrifice animals in the Temple.

I can try to imagine it. I can even pretend I am there. But I still bump up against a disconnect with actual reality. Because mine is a modern world of cars and industry, of cities and electricity, of contemporary clothes and comforts, of airplanes and space exploration. And no matter what I do, I cannot fake out my consciousness entirely, and *really* believe I am there.

Can the gospel come alive in my world too?

I need to pull up the top cellophane sheet of my image slate once again and erase all past preconceptions so that I can start fresher yet...closer...more immediate. I need to bring the gospel into this world where I live, rather than artificially trying to force myself back into a world of which I know so little.

I need to ask, not merely what it was like for the people of first-century Palestine when an astonishing man appeared among them...I need to ask what it would be like for such a man to appear suddenly in *my* life, a man I have never seen before, never heard of, whom I know nothing about.

Where are you at this moment...right now as you read?

Pause...look up, about, and into the world around you.

What kind of setting is it? What do you see—the interior of an office, a campus, a residential district outside your window? Open countryside perhaps meets your eye, or a busy city street, a crowded subway or airport, the interior of your bedroom or living room or kitchen. Maybe you are seated in a library, a retirement home, a cafe or cafeteria or factory lunchroom.

What would it be like if Jesus suddenly walked into the midst of your world? Not in a white glowing robe, but looking like any other person, perhaps in a business suit. Would you leave everything to follow Him?

I happen to be looking out toward a stormy Pacific Ocean at this moment. We all live somewhere, and as I happen to live on the coast of northern California, on most days, even when I travel, I can see the ocean. Right now I am away from home about two hours north in southern Oregon. I am seated comfortably with paper and pen...actually, I am writing this very book.

The water's edge is about two hundred yards from where I sit. Gray menacing waves are crashing on a beach that at the moment looks very unfriendly. A small RV park with a few trailers sits to the left of my vantage point, past which a low ridge of sand covered with scruffy beach grasses and a few stunted fir and spruce, separates it from the sea and parallels the shoreline for about a mile. Mingled with the sound of the waves, I can occasionally hear the traffic of the busy north-south highway about 50 yards behind me. Along both sides of this thoroughfare are located the motels and schools and stores, office buildings and restaurants, of this small coastal town. Out in the water a little way to the north, boats bob about where they are moored in the harbor. After last night's storm, the fishermen are waiting for a break in the weather.

That is where I am. Where are *you*?

We are all somewhere in today's world right now.

I think it would help each one of us to envision what it might be like if today, in the midst of our daily schedules—on your campus, in your office, out the window of your home, in the midst of city traffic and noise, in the room in which I am seated, or out the window where you—

Wait just a minute...

Something is going on over there...out on one of the grassy dunes I was just telling you about beyond the RV park. I can't quite tell what...I see some people...yes, now it looks like a small gathering is walking away from those trailers across the sand.

I'm going to see if I can get a closer look...

It's just a few moments later. I'm at the window and it is just as I thought.

There seems to be a man in front, walking up the grassy incline toward the beach with 10 or 12, maybe 15 people following him. But now I'm seeing more people coming out of the trailers and chasing after them to catch up. A few people have built a small fire out of driftwood on the beach—the wind is blowing this way and I can just faintly catch a whiff of the smoke...but they're leaving it now and are running after him too.

I can't tell from here what it's all about...maybe it's something to do with a group staying in their RVs together. But no...now people who have been walking along the water's edge looking for agates are hurrying over to join them too. It's probably 20 or 25 now. I am seeing people moving toward this little group from all directions, from up and down the beach, from across the dunes. The man in front is walking along in no hurry, but despite his apparent calm the swarm of people around him is growing rapidly.

I see both men and women...and now that I look more closely there are a lot of children too. Now people are pouring out of the trailer park...they must have all heard something...it's becoming almost a frenzy.

He's made his way over the grassy dune and is walking along the beach...everyone following. I can just manage to see them over the top of the rise of sand.

Now he has stopped. He's talking to a few men at the water's edge near where some of the fishing boats are tied up...local fishermen, I assume. Perhaps they're talking about the potential catch during a stormy winter like this.

Now he's on the move again. Several of the men he was just talking to have joined in and are walking along too, although it looks like they left behind some of the nets and equipment they had been working on. Something very unusual is going on, but—

They're almost out of my sight...no, the man just turned. He is coming back over the sand on a little pathway that leads toward the streets of the town and the highway. I'm going outside for a better look. I'll grab my pen and notebook so I can keep track of what's happening...no time to turn out the lights or lock up...I've got to catch up with the crowd and see what's going on!

I'm outside now…the throng has reached the main street about a quarter mile from me. I'm running to get up to the trailing fringes as it heads toward the middle of town.

It's really remarkable. There are so many people! It's not just the trailer park people and those from the beach, they're pouring out of motels and stores. Up ahead there's a school…hundreds of kids are flooding out. They may have to cancel classes for the rest of the day.

Nobody is even trying to keep on the sidewalk now…the commotion is spilling onto the street. All around me people are saying they've never seen anything like it.

When the man left the seashore there were probably 50 or 75 following. I now estimate the crowd at three hundred…and growing fast.

Everyone is curious…pandemonium is setting in. More and more are running up to join the throng, in tens and twenties, not just ones and twos!

A small group is clustered in a circle around him as he walks. I think he is talking to them, but there is so much noise and hubbub I haven't an idea what he might be saying.

He's walking through the business district now…the crowd has grown to a throng—five…six…maybe seven hundred. They're streaming out of stores and office buildings and grocery stores and cafes…past the small hospital and eye clinic…doctors and patients are pouring out, some still in green hospital gowns looking sick and feeble, but expectant. Traffic is backing up…the streets are filling with people. Nobody can go anyplace. All of downtown is congested.

I'm doing my best to press forward through the madness, but not having much luck. I've got to get closer so I can get a better look and find out what has everyone so excited.

It's a few minutes later. It's grown to over a thousand people now…it's huge…the whole town has virtually shut down.

Bumping and crowding about me on every side I hear people abuzz with questions. *"Who is he?"* they're saying. *"What's it all about…have you heard what he said…where are we going?"*

No one seems to know any more than I do, or why this multitude is following the man that started it all. Most are tagging along out of curiosity. How can you see something like this and not jump up and follow? The minute I saw people running, my curiosity was aroused...I couldn't help wanting to see what it was about.

We're past the business district and have reached the outskirts of town now...the crowd continues to surge slowly along.

"He's moving toward that hill on old Zeb's property on the other side of the highway," I hear someone say.

In the distance, other voices and shouts raise themselves above the roar of the crowd.

"There's going to be a speech..."

"He's about to tell us what's going on..."

I hear a few people talking about hurrying home to grab some lunch first and then coming back for the speech.

I'm still trying to squeeze my way through. I'm getting closer to the man...I still can't see quite all the way to the front where the small group surrounds him.

A minute or two more has gone by...

I'm beginning to catch sight of the inner circle....they are listening intently. Yes, there are a few of the local fishermen just as I thought, along with a three-piece suit type—a banker or lawyer perhaps—several women, two or three laborers, a teacher I think, someone wearing a uniform who looks to be a government official, and several others. I can't tell much about them.

I'm getting a few glimpses of the man himself...

He looks ordinary enough. Nothing remarkable that I can see. Certainly nothing that explains all this. He's not movie-star handsome—medium build, light brown hair ruffled a little and blowing in the gentle breeze, average features. He's dressed casually, not in a business suit—simple denim trousers, long-sleeved blue wool button-down shirt, and outdoor walking shoes. He's no one famous that I've ever seen.

He is talking, gesturing about occasionally, to the men and women with him. His face is serious, though not stern. They must be discussing something important. They are hanging on his every word? I can barely hear his voice.

I'm still trying to inch closer to see if—

He is slowing. Now he has ceased to move altogether.

Those next to him come to a halt. Gradually the whole multitude bumps to a standstill.

He has stopped talking.

Expecting something, the crowd grows silent.

Slowly the man turns around. Now for the first time I see his face clearly. It is a surprising face, not for its features...but for its expression. But I have little time to ponder it.

He is scanning the multitude...looking for something...looking for someone in the midst of the vast throng. Slowly his head pans back and forth.

Then his gaze comes to rest.

A chill sweeps through my body. All of a sudden I am aware he has found what he is searching for.

He is looking straight at me!

All around, the crowd that was pressed so close begins silently to move away from where I am standing. Slowly everyone backs further and further...until I am left alone.

No one is within 20 feet of me. I feel exposed, vulnerable, naked. More than a thousand silent stares are resting upon me.

The intensity of the man at the center of this frenzy is most penetrating of all. For he too is silent...his gaze riveted toward me.

Our eyes meet.

I am rooted to where I stand, trembling, goosebumps crawling over my arms and neck. I have no idea what this is all about. I had only been one of a thousand others a moment before. Suddenly I find myself at the heart of the uproar. The man's friends are staring at me too...waiting to see what I will do.

How long we remain like this, his eyes probing my very soul, I don't know.

The crowd continues hushed. The whole town stands still. Perhaps, as far as I know, the whole world.

There I stand like a statue, the man's eyes boring into mine.

13

Then I perceive that he is about to speak. He does not exactly smile, but his expression is warm, friendly, inviting. I sense that he knows me, that he has known me all the while...even as I first sat watching from a distance...knowing that he would walk within sight of my window, knowing that I would look up and see him...and knowing that I would drop what I was doing and follow.

At last he nods imperceptibly, gestures with his hand to indicate that he wants me to walk forward and join him.

Finally he speaks. Everyone probably hears, for it is so quiet. But I know his words are meant for my ears alone. Perhaps I should say they are meant for my heart.

"I want you to come with me," he says.

Then he turns and begins walking again in the direction he had been going before.

Still stunned that I have been singled out from among so many, what can I do but what he says? By now I have completely forgotten how quickly I had dropped what I was doing to hurry after him, leaving the lights on and the door unlocked. I have forgotten my book, my schedule, my plans for the day.

How can one not follow? His presence is so commanding, so full of authority.

How can we not go with him, you and I? For he has spoken to us both. Who wouldn't run along at first to see what it is all about—you leaving your comfortable homes and offices and schools and factories and churches and businesses...me jumping up from where I sat and leaving my work behind.

Yes, I followed...from a distance...gradually moving closer...trying to learn more.

But then suddenly I am no mere spectator.

He has found me in the midst of the multitude. His eyes have locked into mine.

And he has said, "Come with me."

14

I *want* to follow…want to be part of it, though I still don't even know what I am being drawn into. It seems there is no place else to be, no place that one would want to be than here…with him.

I hesitate only a moment, then hasten forward at a half-run to join the circle of those closest beside him. The multitude closes around again.

It doesn't occur to me until sometime later that I still don't know the man's name.

Three

Questions at Night

DARKNESS HAS FALLEN.

My mind is full.

Many perplexities present themselves. Though it has only been a little over 24 hours since I followed the crowd out into the street and found myself suddenly face-to-face with the man at the center of the storm, so much in my life has changed.

No doubt you had the same reaction as you rose from where you were seated, and likewise left your home or place of work to follow the multitude. You were caught up in it just as suddenly and unexpectedly as was I.

I don't know what to make of it all. He says such unusual things. What does it all mean?

I don't exactly even know who he is.

His closest friends call him *Teacher* and *Master*. Occasionally he refers to himself as the *Son of Man*, whatever that means. It is an odd expression.

Of course by now I know that his given name is Jess. But no one seems to use that for address. Neither do they call him by his last name, *Josephson*, as would seem customary.

Therefore, as I follow to discover what his teachings about God mean in my life, I don't know what I should call him. But I am a little timid to ask. He never rebukes anyone for a question. He is always very patient to answer. Yet I am hesitant to speak out and perhaps betray my foolishness.

And now as night closes in, I am left alone with my thoughts...my uncertainties...my doubts.

The hour grows late. Still sleep eludes me.

Faintly through the open window I hear voices, speaking softly and in hushed tones. I rise to glance out.

Two figures are walking amongst the trees outside, near where we are staying.

It is him!

In haste I dress, quickly leave the room, hurry down the stairs as quietly as possible so as to disturb none of the others. Reaching the cool still air of night, I glance about, then follow in the direction I last saw them.

A partial moon hangs in the sky to faintly guide my steps. I move slowly into the depths of a park. Gradually soft voices come into hearing. I creep forward, straining to listen, pausing at length behind a tree at the edge of the clearing where the two men have seated themselves on a bench and are talking quietly together.

Scattered words from their discussion drift toward me.

"...born again...see the Kingdom of God."

"How...when he is old...a second time?"

"I tell you the truth—" begins Jess, then pauses.

He glances up, exactly in the direction where I am standing. As before, with uncanny intuition, he senses my presence.

He rises and walks forward. No annoyance registers on his face, but rather a smile of invitation.

"Please, my friend," he says, approaching with outstretched hand, "come join us. You are most welcome."

I step out of the shadows, feeling a momentary twinge of embarrassment. But quickly it passes. He leads me across the dewy grass to the bench where the other sits waiting, a man I recognize from among the throng the day before. We greet one another and shake hands.

"Nick and I were just discussing how one participates in God's life and lives in His Kingdom," says Jess, resuming his seat as I sit down on the other side. "Perhaps you have found yourself puzzled about it too."

"Actually, yes...I have," I reply. "I have been listening to you since yesterday, when...you know...when you said you wanted me to follow you."

He nods.

"And afterward, when you were speaking from the little knoll when we were gathered in the field...when you were telling us what brings happiness in life."

"Did you understand what I said?" he asks.

"Mostly, I think."

"But still you are perplexed?"

"I don't know...somewhat perhaps."

I falter. It is difficult to open my mind to him. Somehow I sense that he already knows what I want to say.

"It's just...you see," I go on hesitantly, "I have been a religious person for some time, most of my life actually."

I pause for a breath. These are difficult thoughts to express.

"I'm not a saint by any means," I continue. "I know I've got problems like anyone else. But I have tried to be a good and decent person. And yet everything you are saying about God and the Kingdom, about repentance, about hungering after righteousness...it is much different than what I have been accustomed to hearing in church."

"You are right," Jess replies. "The Kingdom of God is not about being religious. Nor is it a way of life taught in church."

"What is it then?"

"It is about doing God's will."

"I have heard about God's will all my life. But it sounds so different when you say it, so down to earth and practical. What is God's will exactly?"

"That is what I have been sent to tell you and show you."

"Sent? By whom...God?"

"Yes. God—our Father in Heaven."

"How does one live in His Kingdom, then...how does one begin?" I ask.

"That is just what I have been explaining to Nick. To enter into the Kingdom of God you must be born again."

"But how can that be? Surely you don't mean actually to be *born* a second time."

"Yes," he replies, "but a spiritual second birth, not a physical one as was your first. That was a birth created by your father and mother. The birth I speak of is one created by the Father and Holy Spirit."

"Who is the Holy Spirit?"

19

"I will explain everything in time," he replies with a smile. "For now I only want you to see the necessity of this second birth."

"What comprises such a spiritual birth, then?"

"Deciding to live in God's Kingdom and do His will."

"That does not sound complicated."

"It is not. It is only difficult for those who want their own will instead of God's."

I try to take in his words. They seem straightforward. Yet somehow I sense that they contain depths and mysteries it will take me a lifetime to apprehend.

"For those who love God and want to do as He tells them," Jess goes on, "nothing could be easier than such a second birth—making the decision to live according to His will."

"But why do you liken it to a birth?"

"Because mankind is born into the world wanting to please only himself. His will is entirely a self-will. Such is the bent of humanity's fallen nature. It comes with the first birth. Surely you see it in yourself—the predisposition to put yourself first, to satisfy only yourself, even occasionally to do what you know is wrong."

"Yes...I am aware of it," I nod a little sheepishly.

"This self-will is the curse of Adam's race. A second birth, therefore—a spiritual birth—is necessary in order to lay down that self-will, and take up God's will instead. To leave the life of self-rule behind and be born into a new life where God rules."

I am doing my best to understand.

"That is why I say you must be born again," Jess says, "born *out* of self-will *into* God's will. It is a birth of relinquishment—laying down the one to take up the other."

I ponder his words a few moments. At my side, Nick is also thoughtful.

"Then what is this will of God you speak of?" I ask after a few moments. "I want to live in it."

"Have patience," he answers. "I will show you. Listen to what I say. Heed my teaching. Follow my example. Then you will know how to lay down your own and live in God's will."

I nod again. I sense that the opportunity for questions on this night for me is done. The time has come for me to listen, as he said, to heed his teaching, and to follow his example.

Gradually he and Nick resume their conversation.

Nick is filled with many questions about what Jess is talking about, as am I. I sit and listen patiently as he seeks to explain it.

I must confess that I understand only snatches of what follows. It is new and some of it sounds strange in my ears. One portion of the discussion, however, remains with me after that night, and continues to repeat itself in my mind ever since. I cannot claim to fully grasp its import. But I find the words comforting and reassuring in the midst of the many questions that remain.

Jess said that his Father in Heaven loved the world so much that He sent His only Son to earth, to lead people into His Kingdom and show them how to do His Father's will. Then he said that they who believe in the Son—those who enter God's Kingdom and do His will—shall never die. They will live with God forever. Their life in His Kingdom will be eternal.

It begins to dawn on me that when he speaks of God's Son, he means himself.

But I do not understand what this signifies.

Four

Upside-down Kingdom

I DECIDE TO ACCOMPANY HIM WHEN HE LEAVES THE PLACE where I first went out to meet him. He and his friends are on the move again—walking, traveling, venturing by boat up one of the rivers or along the shore. I am one of them now. A small crowd still accompanies us. Some come and go, others follow in cars and vans.

The days are long and tiring. He is teaching many things, preaching occasionally to the multitudes, often drawing his closest companions aside in a house or perhaps to some lonely place in the country where we talk quietly amongst ourselves. At such times he always encourages discussion. I am beginning to realize just how much there is for me to learn. Whole lifetimes of wrong attitudes and bad habits and poor choices must be reoriented in new directions.

All of us have many questions. His teaching, though simple in one way, is also new and profound.

He tells us to do good to those who wrong us, to pray for our enemies, to return evil with kindness, and in all circumstances to do good toward others. Such concepts cut across the grain of our humanity at every turn. He speaks of putting to death whatever rises up urging us to place ourselves ahead of another, of giving up what we have been accustomed to thinking of as our rights...and doing so every day and in all circumstances.

Elevating the interests of others above one's own is everything to him. Over and over he emphasizes that treating others as you would have them treat you is the gauge by which to measure behavior.

It is a high standard! Who can possibly do such a thing? Yet that is the essence of his message. He says this is the beginning of what comprises life in God's Kingdom. Without such simple kindness and courtesy, there can be no spirituality. Doctrinal rightness matters nothing, he says. How you treat others and how you respond to God, matter everything.

He speaks as though it is the most natural way in the world for men and women to think and behave toward one another. He says the human heart was created to put others first, but because of sin has forgotten how. Sin spoiled what God created. That is why we must repent—for turning away from God's purpose—and leave our sin. He is teaching us how to go back to that original will in which we were created to live.

I am beginning to grasp why he has been stressing the necessity of being born anew. For surely this life he teaches is as unfamiliar to the spiritual senses of attitude, response, and choice, as was the world of noise and light to our physical senses when we emerged from the wombs of our mothers.

He speaks of the self—that part of one's being that exalts itself above others and above God—as the great enemy of God's purpose. God's will cannot be known and lived, he says, without laying down that which opposes it—the will of one's own flesh...one's own self-will.

Sin, he says, is nothing more than wanting what *you* want instead of what God wants, and thinking and acting according to that wrong motive.

He gives numerous examples of how this pattern is to be reversed, how we are to respond in an opposite manner from the natural inclination of self-will. Such as—don't retaliate if someone strikes you, give more than you are asked for, show mercy, rejoice and forgive when wrong is done you, don't get angry, do good deeds in such a way that people don't see them, do more than required, pray in private, don't worry, trust God to supply your needs, don't judge others, and make no show of spirituality.

They are such common, everyday things. It is difficult at first to see why they are so important.

He always adds, however, that life in God's Kingdom is not comprised of obeying a list of such things. It cannot be done, he stresses, without a total shift in attitude. Neither can it be done halfway. It takes a

24

change of heart, a whole new way of viewing life. That is why one must be born again, he says, in order to enter into this new life. One must turn from the old way—putting one's *own* will first—and abandon oneself by a decision of choice, into God's will. Without such a fundamental change, the life he describes is impossible.

It is not the same as turning over a new leaf, or making a new year's resolution to "do a little better." It is a complete new birth into a different way of life, from which there is no turning back. He often says, "Count the cost. Don't come with me unless you are prepared to see it through."

What he teaches of such a life is nothing more than what he does himself. He finds selflessness not difficult in the least. It is a joy to him to serve those around him. He continually seeks opportunity to serve. When someone speaks rudely to him—and incredible as it seems, the church and synagogue officials are rudest of all—he smiles and speaks kindly in return. Never have I seen a mean-spirited reaction rise on his face. Forgiveness with him is instantaneous. I do not think it would be possible to hurt his feelings. I have seen him sad, but never offended. His heart is too full of forgiveness to be offended. He is always the last to drink when we come to a stream or water fountain. More often than not, he serves us at mealtime. And he always speaks graciously and courteously. When you are with him, you know he cares about you. You feel that he likes you. More than that—you know that he loves you. How can one not love him in return? He is a remarkable man...a good man...a pleasant man. Is it any wonder we are drawn to him?

This must be why he says we are to follow his example. Were I not witnessing him living the life he speaks of with my own eyes, surely I would think it impossible.

It is curious, however, how lacking in religious form and dogma is his teaching. I keep expecting him to outline more specific doctrine. But there has been no hint of it yet.

He seems especially to avoid pious types. There are only two or three ministers in our group, two priests, and one Jewish rabbi.

Usually when clerics and religious leaders come around, his manner changes imperceptibly. He does not become stern exactly, but it is clear he dislikes spiritualized jargon and puffed-up piety. With such men and women he cuts immediately to practicalities of service—sometimes abruptly—and instructs them to carry out some act of kindness. Often they are taken aback and offended, thinking no doubt that they should have been brought into his circle of leadership.

A certain pastor, expensively dressed and proud of his five thousand-member congregation, his many books, and his nationwide television ministry, was such a one who went away highly offended at the treatment he had received which was unworthy, as he saw it, of his lofty calling. There are reports circulating that this man has gone to others and that they are planning a protest against what they are now calling a grassroots cult. Apparently there are a growing number like him who are angry at the effect this teaching is having on the people in their churches.

But Jess looks for humility in those to whom he delegates responsibility. With him, all is upside-down to how things function in the world. Authority is upside-down. Ministry is upside-down. Significance is upside-down.

One of his favorites is a great burly fisherman, a man who must occasionally watch the outbursts of his tongue because of habits long ingrained from a hard life at sea. But he is learning rapidly, and Jess seems to take special delight in the gradual softening we all observe in him.

There is also a prostitute among us. Her presence put a number of people off at first. But her tears of remorse for what she once was are never far from the surface. Most have come by now to accept her, and are gentle toward her. As with the fisherman, Jess is very tender, and speaks with unusual compassion whenever she is near.

Much of the group is made up of ordinary working men and women, some educated, some not. We have been a little surprised that we haven't once gone to church together. He treats Saturday and Sunday like all other days. Every day, he says, is God's day.

As we travel further from the city, the crowd gradually dissipates. At first, when they thought something new was going on, they poured out from everywhere to find out what it was. But when they learn that he is speaking quietly about how to live, they do not find it so exciting as they hoped.

I think many expect music and impassioned worship services. When they hear that a crowd is gathering, musicians flock in by the dozen, like some of the pastors I suppose, thinking that they will be asked to perform. They are surprised to see no guitars, instruments, or sound equipment. They can't believe that there is no band, or that we do not even have a music team. Of course, they are quick to offer their services, going straight to Jess to tell him of the leading they feel to share their music with the body. He smiles, tells them to take their instruments home, and then come back and follow him. These soon leave, disappointed at how little regard he has for their talents. Most of them I have not seen again, although one or two have done as he said.

So gradually most of the throngs have lost interest and have gone back to their homes and jobs and churches.

He often pauses and looks out over the people who come and go with a compassionate longing, a sad expression. He knows what he has to give them. But he also knows that he cannot give it unless they want it. Self-satisfaction, he tells us, is the root of all stagnation in life, adding that self-importance is the cause of stagnation in the church. This truth is so easy to see in the number of church people who come once or twice, and then leave unimpressed and uninspired. That is why he says that only those who hunger and thirst after righteousness will be blessed and satisfied.

On the few occasions when he pauses and turns, as he did to me, and looks into the crowd with the eyes of invitation and command, the men and women he calls come forward, as I did, to join the little band. He only seems to invite those whom he knows are ready to begin living in this upside-down Kingdom whose life principles he has come to share.

And so gradually, though the crowds have largely disbursed, the group of his close followers has slowly grown.

Five

A Woman at a Market

W E COME AFTER A FEW DAYS TO A SMALL TOWN IN THE HILLS away from the coast.

No one seems to know him there. No throng pours out to greet us. We enter the town unobserved. It is about noon.

We stop at the town square near a small mini-market and sit down to rest. We have been traveling for some distance and are all tired and hungry.

"I will go and see what we can get for lunch," says Andy, one of the fishermen.

"Here's a market right here," says one.

"I feel like fish and chips," says Andy, moving away.

"I'll join you," says Pete, his brother, the large man I mentioned before. Several others also chime in. Finally the rest of us decide to go along too.

"Stay here, Master," adds Pete. He is always looking for a chance to return Jess's kindness toward him. "We will find food and bring it back here. You rest. I can see that you are tired from the journey."

Jess nods with a smile and thanks him. Then we all head off in what we take to be the direction of the market.

I am the first to return. I find him, as is often the case, talking with someone at the square. A woman, probably 40 or 45, dark-skinned, very attractive though graying noticeably, is seated on a bench beside him. They are both holding plastic bottles of water, which I assume the woman bought at the nearby market. She is listening intently to Jess. Despite her

29

beauty, she appears to have had a difficult life. She does not appear happy, but careworn. In her eyes I see the look I often notice in those to whom he turns when speaking to a crowd—an expression of hunger in the eyes. He seems drawn to such individuals like a magnet.

I approach.

He glances up with a smile and gestures for me to join them. He is always open, and never pushes one of us away no matter whom he is with.

"This woman and I have been talking," he says as he introduces us. "She wonders why I am speaking with her since we are of different religions. Actually," he adds with a light laugh, "I asked her if I could have one of her bottled waters, for I was very thirsty. I think my question surprised her, didn't it, my dear?"

She nods, returning his smile.

"So what would you tell her?" he says, turning to me. "Is what I have been teaching you a new religion that includes some but excludes those of different faith, perhaps such as she?"

"No," I reply, glancing toward the woman. She is watching to see what I will say. "I would not even call it a religion at all," I add, "but a way of life."

"You have answered well," Jess replies.

He turns again to the woman. "You see, it is exactly as I have been telling you," he says. "The water of life I offer is for men and women of *all* religions, even people of no religion. It is not a religion at all, as my friend has just told you, but a new way to live as sons and daughters of our heavenly Father."

"But are all people God's sons and daughters?" she asks.

"Of course," he replies. "He made all mankind in his image."

"I thought only certain chosen people, such as what some call the elect—"

"Religions that exclude do not come from God," he answers before she finishes her statement. "All men and women were created by the same God for the same purpose—to live in harmony with him as his children. But sin caused mankind to walk away from that life of harmony, and choose instead a life of independence, thinking such would make them happy."

He pauses briefly.

"Has it made you happy?" he adds.

She glances down, embarrassed it seems.

"No," she whispers quietly.

"It never does," says Jess tenderly. "It is impossible for independence from God to make people happy, for they were created to live in sonship. That is why I have come, that men and women like you, my dear, might regain that life, and experience it abundantly. That is why they must learn to drink of new waters. Only so can they again become God's sons and daughters."

"And can *all* drink of these waters you speak of," she says, "even an Arab like me?"

"All can. All must. All will," replies Jess. "It is living water, far more refreshing even than this bottled spring water we have been drinking—living water for your soul. When you drink of this water," he says, lifting the bottle in his hand, "you will thirst again. But when your soul drinks of the living water that I give, it will never thirst again."

"What you say is so difficult to understand," she says. "Our religion does not teach such things."

"That is because it is a man-made religion, not a way of life," replies Jess. "But it is not so difficult if you would know your Father in Heaven," he goes on. "Once you decide to be His daughter and drink from the waters of His life, those waters will well up within and give you eternal life. You may indeed be an Arab. What is that to God? I am His son, you are His daughter. He wants us to live as His obedient and faithful children."

"Then please," she says, "give me this living water to drink."

"First, I would like you to go get your husband and bring him back. I want to speak with him also."

"I have no husband," she says.

Jess nods. "I know," he replies, and we detect sadness in his voice. "You have had five husbands, and are now living with a sixth and are not even married to him."

The woman's face turns ashen. She is stunned at what he has said. I find myself shocked as well. How could he have known?

31

"I...I—you are right...forgive me," she says softly, glancing again at the ground. It is silent a moment. Then she looks up, tears glistening in her eyes. "Who *are* you?" she asks.

Jess merely returns her gaze with a smile.

"You...you are surely a man sent from God," she goes on. "I know there is one who is supposed to come, a great man, a prophet. I have always been taught that he would make things clear, and explain everything to us about God. But...but you..."

Just then a clamor of voices and footsteps behind us intrudes into my ears.

I look around to see the others returning with food and drink. I turn back again a moment later to the woman seated on the bench. An expression of astonishment has spread over her face. Her eyes are open wide in wonder.

But I do not hear what Jess has just said to her.

Six

Many Reactions

WHILE WE EAT LUNCH, THE WOMAN RUNS EXCITEDLY BACK INTO TOWN and begins telling everyone what has happened. She is in such a hurry that she leaves her water bottle still sitting on the bench.

Meanwhile, as we enjoy what Pete and Andy and the others have bought, Jess compares his teaching about the Kingdom of God to the food we are eating, just like he had called it living water when speaking to the woman. Some are confused about what he says, wondering if the woman had given him something to eat while they had been away at the fish and chip stand.

While he is still trying to explain his meaning, saying that even more important to him than physical food to sustain his body is the food to his spirit of doing the will of God, people from the town come flocking out to see him. By later that afternoon a huge crowd has gathered. Since it is new to them, he teaches many of the same things we have heard several times already.

We remain there two days, and a number from that region believe and afterward come with us.

We leave, and make our way slowly back toward the coast. As we go he teaches us many things.

Word begins to go ahead of us that we are coming, such that whenever we come near any town or village, great crowds are already gathered, including many sick and lame and blind, hoping to be healed. Many have been healed already by his touch, and many demonic afflictions cured.

33

Sometimes they have been waiting for us a long time and are faint with hunger, not sure when we will arrive and not wanting to leave. Food and provision for such crowds is occasionally a problem as he is now avoiding the larger towns because of the growing opposition by religious officials. Most of the places where people go out to see him, therefore, are far from their homes. Since we are near the coast, however, bread and smoked salmon are usually plentiful. Most are willing and eager to share.

We have been especially curious to observe the great variety of response to his teaching even though he speaks the same message to all.

The most frequent points he makes are these: That the time has arrived for the Kingdom of God to be lived on the earth. Then he calls his hearers to repent of their self-will and independence from God, urging them to be born into God's Kingdom by believing in the good news about life as His sons and daughters.

Why, then, do some, like those of us with him, receive that message and follow eagerly?

But why do others seem they have not heard at all, as if they are completely deaf to his words?

Why do some follow for a short time, then return home?

And why do still others go away angry at what they hear, such as the televangelist who is rallying opposition in the city even now?

Puzzled, one day I ask him about it.

He does not answer immediately, but looks out to where a farmer on his tractor is planting a new crop in a freshly ploughed brown field. A serious expression comes over his face, and at length he begins to speak.

"Do you see that farmer over there?" he says. "He is sowing seed throughout his entire field. But all of it will not grow as he hopes. Some will fall along the edges and the birds will come and eat it. Other seed will fall where the ground is rocky and the soil shallow. Other seed will get blown into that adjoining pasture where his cows are grazing. There it will be choked and unable to grow and bear grain. Only a portion of the seed will root deeply into the good soil, and then come up to bear an abundant crop. Pay attention to what you hear."

When we are alone later, we continue discussing the story he had told and again ask him about it. I had begun noticing recently that his

34

questions are becoming more and more probing, that he expects more from us, that his teaching is deepening and is hard to understand. On this occasion he looks around at us with an expression of urgency and expectation, as if he is perhaps a little frustrated at our need to keep asking such simple questions.

"Come, listen," he says. "The secret of the Kingdom of God has been given to you, because you have hungered after it and have followed me to learn of it. But for the crowds, much is confusing and is in parables. They block their own understanding by their self-satisfaction. Thus they are ever hearing but never perceiving. If you cannot understand this simple parable, how will you be able to understand all I have to teach you. So here is its meaning.

"The farmer sows the seed as I am sowing the Word of God. He plants his seed in the ground. I plant God's truths in the hearts of those who listen. But the seed does not strike the same root within all, for all are not hungry for the truth.

"Some people are like the seed scattered on the path. As soon as they hear it, satan comes and takes it away by whispering words of independence and self-satisfaction in their ear.

"Others, like the seed sown on rocky places, hear the Word and at once receive it gladly. But they have no root. Their response comes from emotion and the lust for experience rather than obedience. Therefore, when difficulties come and when obedience is demanded, they quickly lose interest and fall away.

"Still others, like the seed sown among thorns, hear the Word and want to receive it. But the lure of the world, the deceitful attraction of wealth, and the pressure of false attitudes and values in their friends around them choke out the Word in their hearts, making it unable to grow.

"Finally, like seed planted in good soil, there are those who hear the Word, accept it, step obediently into the sonship of their calling, and produce a crop of good for the Kingdom of God—thirty, sixty, and a hundredfold."

"Why is it so?" I ask. "Why do not all want to live an abundant life in God's Kingdom?"

"Because not all want to live as His sons and daughters. Life in the Kingdom means becoming a child. Most people spend their entire lives in a hurry to grow up, trying to grow *out* of childhood, striving for the independence of their adulthood, never realizing that true maturity comes only in laying the right to that independence down so that he or she might become a child again. Now at last comes the opportunity to become a *true* child, a child of childlikeness in the Kingdom, a child by choice not necessity. Sadly, however, this divine sonship and divine daughterhood is not the highest goal of most men and women. Clinging to what they suppose is their right to self-rule, they squander life's greatest privilege and highest opportunity. Thus they achieve the independence they seek, but lose the contentment they hoped to gain.

There can be no Life in self-rule. Nor does any human being have the right to it. But God will not coerce them, though He will do all He can to help them see that such is the only way to bear fruit and reap a full harvest in life."

It falls silent as we reflect on the teaching.

"Consider carefully what you hear," Jess adds at length. "For if you understand and act upon what you know of God's truth, more truth will be given you, and your wisdom will increase. But do not forget Solomon's legacy. If you do not obey the truth that is given you, even the understanding you have will be taken away. Obedience is the only door into the temple of wisdom."

Seven

The Wealthy
Young Evangelist

WE COME INTO ONE OF THE LARGER CITIES OF THE REGION.

By now the opposition is growing so strong that its leaders, politicians, and officials are following our movements carefully. Often when Jess tries to speak to the people, one of them steps forward and raises an issue intended to trick him into a contradictory statement, thinking to discredit him in the eyes of the people.

But they are never successful. They come with thorny theological dilemmas—divorce, authority, taxes, the afterlife, and so on. But Jess perceives their motives too clearly to fall into their traps, then turns their questions back on them with practicalities impossible to dispute.

Jess knows God's heart. It is impossible to sidetrack him with doctrinal debates. Whatever the query, he always remains focused on the purpose of God, whom now more and more he refers to as his Father.

This makes the people love him, and of course inflames the anger of his opponents all the more. Occasionally they can be heard amongst themselves. "We have got to put an end to this, whatever it takes!"

The televangelist has been joined in his effort by several protestant ministers, a high-ranking Catholic cardinal from Rome, a best-selling prophetic writer, and, from what we hear, a leading orthodox rabbi who has come all the way from Jerusalem.

After one of these heated exchanges, in which they ask him if divorce is lawful in God's eyes, we see a young man approach. I immediately assume him to be one of the church leaders, for he had been standing with them a few moments earlier, though he said nothing during the debate. He is expensively dressed in an impeccable dark brown suit, gold watch on one wrist, gold bracelet on the other, and shoes on his feet that appear as costly as his suit. He is young, however, probably no more than 25 or 26.

As he comes closer, suddenly I recognize him. He is a well-known personality, a speaker of some renown at conferences and retreats. I have seen him a few times on television making guest appearances with other evangelists. He is considered a rising star in the religious community and I have heard that he has a book due out being touted as a sure best-seller.

He hurries to catch us before we leave. All at once to my amazement, he falls on his knees before Jess. He has obviously been touched by what he has been listening to.

Jess pauses. He is moved by the young man's display.

"Stand, my friend," he says. "What may I do for you?"

The young man climbs to his feet, takes a deep breath, then begins.

"I am an elder in the largest church in the city," he says. "In fact," he adds with slight embarrassment, "I came with some of those men back there who were questioning you. But as I listened, a question came to me. Despite my leadership position, I asked myself, what if something is missing. I found myself wondering whether I have been seeking the greatest good in life."

"No one is good but God alone," Jess replies. "If you would seek the ultimate good in life, you must seek Him."

"Yes, I know…I understand," says the young man. "But is there anything else I must do to inherit eternal life, anything I have overlooked, anything lacking in my walk?"

"To enter life, obey the commandments," says Jess simply.

"Which ones?"

"All of them."

"Who can do that?" says the young evangelist in astonishment.

"What else would be the requirement?" rejoins Jess. "God wants you to be His obedient son."

"Don't murder, don't commit adultery, don't steal, speak the truth, honor your father and mother, love your neighbor as yourself—I have kept all these for years."

"You *always* love your neighbor as yourself?" probes Jess.

"Not perfectly," falters the man, "but..."

"How much do you love your neighbor?" says Jess, pressing still further.

"I...I think I am as kind to people as anyone else."

"Is being as good as the next man the level of spirituality you seek—an average spirituality? You asked me if there was *anything* you lacked. I assumed you desired more than a mediocre walk with God."

"Yes...I see what you mean. I would say, then, that...yes, I *do* try to love my neighbor...probably more than most people."

"Then remove that watch on your wrist," says Jess, "and take it and give it to that homeless man over there at the intersection."

The man stares dumbfounded for a moment, then glances toward the man a block away sitting on the sidewalk holding a cardboard sign on which are scrawled the words, "Broke and hungry...please help."

Jess continues to gaze into the young man's eyes, and I see the deep love he feels for him in his heart.

"But..." he says hesitantly, "but he would only go sell it at the nearest pawn shop for a fraction of its value."

"Then go yourself and sell it somewhere else," returns Jess. "Then give the money away to the poor however you like. Then you will have treasure in Heaven. Then come, follow me."

The young man stands, still gaping for a few seconds more, then glances down, slowly turns, and walks away.

Tears gather in Jess's eyes as he watches him go.

"It is hard," he says softly, and only those of us nearest him hear his words, "for those who are attached to their wealth to enter the Kingdom of Heaven."

"Then who can be saved?" Pete asks in astonishment.

"With God all things are possible," replies Jess. "But many who are first will be last, and many who are last will one day be first."

39

We continue on our way. Jess remains subdued over the incident. I think he had truly hoped that the young evangelist would join us. As is usually the way, the rest of us reflect on what had happened. Finally someone asks him about it.

"Were you not a little hard on the young man?" says Pete. "Surely the watch was not so important as to prevent him coming with us."

"That watch must mean a great deal to him," adds Andy.

"Yes, far too much," nods Jess. "The demand I placed on him was not for the watch itself, but for what it represented in his life. He thinks too highly of his gift of oratory and of the praises of men. When he said that he had kept the commandments, he was not far wrong. He is one of the most upstanding, genuinely good men you could hope to meet. He has indeed lived a respectable and godly life. He listed the attributes of righteousness he had kept. But pride is capable of sneaking into the heart even between such commandments. It has begun to do so with him. In the midst of what he considers his righteousness, an invisible stumbling block is rising in the path of deeper obedience. It would always have stood in his way and barred intimacy with the Father."

"But why?" I ask. "How could a simple watch do all that?"

"It was given him as a gift," replies Jess. "He is a dynamic speaker at a young age, highly sought after, and proud of his ability to stir a crowd. That watch was from one of the religious personalities in the city. It is inscribed, 'To a mighty man of God for the next generation.' "

"He is young to be given such praise," I say.

"It is often the way. Young people of talent are raised too high in their own eyes too soon. But he will never be a true man of God until he learns to despise the acclaim of such men as are enamored by his personality rather than his character. He will not become wise until he learns to become a son."

"Was he not in earnest when he came?" I ask.

"He seemed sincere," adds another.

"To a degree he is," replies Jess. "But he is seeking a comfortable discipleship. What he thinks is his spirituality has come far too easily for

40

him. He wants to continue being himself as he is. The humility of a son has not yet been born in him."

"Is that why you had to make such a demand?" I ask.

"Such a crossroad comes to all," replies Jess, "when each has to ask himself how far he wants to go with God. Do they truly want to be a disciple...or only a believer? The young man may be saved, as they are fond of saying. He will get into Heaven. But he has not yet been born into sonship by the relinquishment of his will into the Father's.

"When that moment comes," Jess continues, "I look my followers in the eye—though in truth I am only causing each to look into *himself*—and say, leave all you have and follow me."

"Are possessions evil, then?" Pete asks.

"No," he replies. "It was not the monetary value of the watch itself, nor anything else he owns. All possession comes from God. Everything is His. Money is God's provision for the doing of much good in the world. Had something else been at root of the young man's reluctance to give his all, then that something else, whatever it was, would have been required."

"But must one truly leave *all*?"

"Everyone has *something*," says Jess, "that prevents them giving their entire being to God and laying down their self-will into the will of His Fatherhood. For the church leaders we were speaking with a few minutes ago, it is their self-righteousness. For some it is pride in their theologies. For that dear young man, it happens to be his natural talent and his wealth. When I look in a man's eyes or a woman's eyes, it is always for that thing I look. Because that will always be the one thing standing between them and the fulfillment of their sonship or daughterhood."

"What did you see when you gazed into my eyes?" I ask.

He smiled.

"That you will have to ask the Father to reveal to you," he replies. "But fear not, you have begun to lay it aside already."

Eight

A Question of Identity

WE LEAVE THE CITY.

After a debate about marriage, in which Jess had said that anyone who remarries after divorcing husband or wife commits adultery, the opposition grows all the more heated. Several of the church leaders who had questioned him were themselves in that very situation. It is not a teaching they can tolerate without bringing condemnation upon their own heads, and the heads of half their congregations.

More and more, therefore, Jess is becoming a figure of controversy. Wherever we go, the crowds are filled with discussion and debate between those who receive him gladly and those who are angry about his teaching. The latter insist that as an unmarried man, he has no right to judge those who simply made a mistake by marrying the wrong person. God is a God of forgiveness, they add, who does not condemn them. What right, then, has he to judge them?

A growing number of his opponents can often be seen gathering in clusters about the edges, talking and reasoning among themselves, wearing somber expressions, taking notes, apparently collecting evidence by which to incriminate him. If they can catch him in a statement from which they can make a convincing charge of heresy—along with his inflammatory and unpopular stand on remarriage—they will probably turn the tide of public opinion against him.

The pastors and priests and evangelists and rabbis and authors have ingrained the traditions of their orthodoxies so deeply over so many years, that the people who follow them are paralyzed in constricting straightjackets of religion. They are afraid to question, afraid to think for themselves. Suddenly Jess threatens all that, encouraging people to ask and question and think.

I have heard that two of his statements in particular are being used against him. Jess said, "When I am lifted up, I will draw all men to me." We don't know what he was referring to, but they are using it to advance the claim that he insists all men will enter into eternal life—a clear heresy according to church tradition. Additionally, he frequently likens his relationship with God to that between a father and son. A few days ago he made the declaration, "I and the Father are one." Some of the officials heard his words and seized upon them almost with glee in their eyes. Andy said he heard them leaving excitedly saying, "Now we've got him! He claims equality with God!"

So they have two heresies and the teaching on remarriage to bring against him. And I fear the list of unorthodoxies will grow.

If they can persuade enough public officials to their side, in addition to a growing list of religious leaders, they might even succeed in getting him arrested.

He shows no sign of being afraid of this opposition. He repeatedly says, "The time is not yet come." We assume an eventual showdown is inevitable. What will happen then is anyone's guess.

"Where are we going?" asks Jim as we head north into the country. Jim is one of Andy's close friends who has been with Jess from the first day along the seashore.

"To a remote region," Jess replies. "There are some important things we must talk about together away from the crowds."

"Why away?" asks Jim's brother John.

"Because the opposition you have seen will increase," replies Jess. "There are important truths you must grasp in order to withstand it."

On the way, a few of us begin casually discussing again the many reactions to Jess that we have witnessed. His description of the seed and varying soils has remained fresh in our thinking. We are in a small group some distance ahead of the others.

"One of the reasons people respond so differently," says Pete, "is that they don't know who he is. If they did they would pay more attention."

"You can hardly blame them," adds Jim. "You've got to admit, he is a little cryptic at times."

"Perhaps," rejoins Pete. "But it's obvious from his teaching, isn't it?"

"Maybe not to everyone," I say. "I had my doubts at first too."

"So did I," says Pete. "But still, if they don't know, they shouldn't leave without finding out."

"What about his enemies?" asks Jim.

"Do you think they know?" says John.

"How could they," I add, "with the kinds of things they are saying about him?"

"Maybe it is because they *do* know that they are trying so hard to discredit him," says Andy.

We have not realized that Jess and those he is with have come up behind us. He has been listening to our discussion as we walk. Then I hear his voice.

"So...you think that there is curiosity and uncertainty about me?" he says.

Surprised, I turn to see him nearly in our midst, a smile on his face. A few heads begin to nod in response to his question.

"Well, then, who *do* people say that I am?" he asks.

No one wants to be the first to answer. At length I speak up, since I was the only one present at the time she said it.

"There was that Arab woman," I say. "She thought you might be a prophet."

Now others begin to comment, recounting some of the theories they have heard.

"Most people say you are a good man," says Andy.

"And a great philosopher," adds Jim. "I have heard some compare you to Plato and Socrates."

A light chuckle ripples from his mouth at the thought of it. "Indeed," says Jess, laughing, "that is one I was not aware of. We must have some educated individuals among us."

"I heard a few in that last town calling you a great moral teacher," says John.

Gradually most of the others now throw their thoughts into the discussion.

"The people who knew you—before you closed your workshop, I mean," says someone behind us, "—they simply call you Josephson the carpenter."

Jess smiles. "I do miss working with wood," he says. "It gave me such pleasure. All right, then—what else do they call me? Who else do they think I am?"

"No one knows," says Pete. "You have everyone baffled. They are comparing you to all sorts of men—alive and dead. Some think you are a ghost come back to life."

"I have heard some say you are like Moses," says Andy.

"And Elijah and John the Baptist," puts in another.

"What about that minister who is saying all those things to turn people against you," says Jim. "He thinks you're from the devil."

"He's said as much," adds John. "He calls us a cult."

Slowly it falls silent. We have nearly exhausted the possibilities.

We walk along for some time. No one says a word. I think we begin to sense something important coming.

Finally Jess speaks.

"All right, then," he says, glancing around at each of us in turn. He is no longer smiling. A serious expression is in his eyes and voice. "Who do *you* say that I am?"

The silence deepens. I happen to be at his side at the moment. At length he turns toward me. I see the same expression I had noticed that first day when he scanned the crowd and found me in its midst.

But now his eyes probe even more deeply. I know he is waiting to see what I have learned since that fateful day.

At last I speak. The eyes of the others are also upon me.

"You are," I say slowly, "the Son of God."

Jess takes in the words solemnly, then slowly nods.

"For you to grasp this truth," he says after a moment, "is why you have come out away from the crowds to be alone. But do not yet tell anyone this."

Nine

A Son of My Father

We ARE STILL IN A REMOTE REGION.

Now, however, Jess makes sure no crowds can interrupt our solitude together. I feel a heaviness descending. It is clear that much remains on his mind to tell us after the day's momentous discussion.

That night we check into a bed and breakfast. There are no other guests. The quiet mood deepens at dinner and throughout the evening. I sense that the day's revelation has brought a turning point.

Jess retires early. The rest of us soon follow.

Early the following morning after breakfast we go out. As we walk he begins to probe and question.

Jess turns first to Pete.

"Pete," he says, "who do men say that I am?"

Pete glances around at the rest of us, momentarily confused by the same question from before.

"Uh...Moses, Elijah, like we talked about yesterday...or John the Baptist," he answers after a moment. "And some say a great teacher or a prophet."

"What about you, Pete?" Jess says, again repeating the question. "Who do you say that I am?"

"You are the Son of God," Pete answers.

We all grow quiet. We have each had a night to ponder the previous day's discussion in the quietness of our own thoughts. And now, hearing the astonishing words again, the import of the revelation strikes awe yet more deeply into our hearts. I believe the truth of the words. But the concept is almost too huge to take in, that this man in our midst, seemingly so normal, like me in so many ways, could actually be God Himself— God's very own Son—that he could actually have been sent to earth from Heaven to tell mankind about the personal and loving God who created us. I am scarcely able to take it in.

As if divining my thoughts, as he always seems to, Jess instantly probes straight to the root of my astonishment and perplexity.

"Do you know what this means?" he says, "when you call me the Son of God?"

Pete is silent. So are the rest of us.

Jess glances around to us one by one, holding each of us by the eye a moment…waiting for a response.

Still, no one speaks.

"It means that I have come in my Father's name, because the Father is greater than I," he says at length. "It means that I am in the Father, and the Father is in me. I will repeat it. Believe me when I say that I am in the Father and God is in me. It means that I am entirely His Son. Therefore, I seek not to please myself, but Him who sent me. I do nothing on my own but speak only what God tells me. The words I say to you are not my own. Rather, it is the Father, living in me, who is speaking to you. Do you understand—I am not my *own*…I am a *Son*."

Another silence settles over us. He has never spoken to us like this, so plainly about the Father. No one has ever spoken about God as he does—as if he is so close, so loving, so intimate, rather than a distant and unapproachable lawgiver. Just as we are trying to accustom ourselves to what his being God's Son means, he throws us into yet more perplexity by speaking as if he and God are so linked as… to be one with each other.

If that is true, then surely the only conclusion to be drawn is that he must be more than just a man.

Again he begins to speak in the midst of our thoughts.

"I have come," he says, "because the world *must* learn that I love the Father and that I do exactly what he commands me. This is the core truth of the universe—my obedience to the Father. But because the world does not know my Father, and because satan, His enemy, controls this world, it does not understand His ways. More than that, the world is against God's ways.

"Therefore," he adds, "sonship also means self-denial and death. Do you hear me, Pete...the rest of you?...death. Death to the world and its values and attitudes and systems and priorities, its ways of thinking. Death to self-will. Death to rights. Death to all that would please the self. Being a son means nothing less than *dying* into the will of the Father."

We listen attentively, but his voice and expression are strange, unlike what we are accustomed to.

"My call upon you is total," he continues. "Why do you think I did not call everyone in the crowd, but singled you out? Because you were ready to leave all and follow me. Most are not prepared for that level of discipleship. They think the call to follow is an invitation to a life of gaiety, emotion, experience, and fellowship. They want to join in because of the crowd, the activity, what looks like fun, thinking I am hosting a celebration.

"No, my friends. I am throwing no party. This is no occasion for revelry. I am leading a funeral procession. Those who come must fall in step beside me toward what will lead to their own death. All who follow must grow ready for that moment when I will look them in the eye a second time, and say, 'Do you know who I am in your life... and to what I call you?' "

Again he pauses to gaze at us seriously.

"If any man or woman," he goes on after a moment, "would come after me, he must deny himself and take up his burden and follow me. For whoever wants to save his life will lose it, but whoever loses his life for me and for God's Kingdom will save it. What good is it for a man to gain the whole world in this adulterous and sinful time, yet lose his own soul? Indeed, what can a man give in exchange for his soul?"

As on many occasions before, his words are heavy with import we but faintly grasp. This time he is silent a long time. We continue walking back to the bed and breakfast as he allows us opportunity to reflect on what he has said. Quietly I return to my room.

We spend three days in that place.

It is unlike anything we have yet experienced together. He continues to teach much about self-denial, rejection, and suffering. I do not know why he is suddenly emphasizing such things. The mood among us continues somber. It is not a pleasing teaching to hear.

I cannot help occasionally wondering what I have gotten myself into.

Ten

What Does Sonship Mean?

At last we prepare to leave our place of solitude and retreat.

To our astonishment he leads south, toward the large city where the opposition is mounting its most vigorous campaign against him.

As our direction becomes obvious, we all grow troubled. We are nervous, for him more than for ourselves. Quietly, in twos and threes, we discuss our concern.

Finally Pete takes him aside. It is usually his way to speak bluntly. Occasionally he blurts out things without thinking.

"Master, what are you doing?" he says. "You cannot actually be thinking of going straight into the city, not the way things stand now. They will...I don't know what they will do—but it can't be good!"

"They will kill me," says Jess calmly. "Is that what you were about to say?"

"I don't know...maybe," fumbles Pete. "All I know is that I don't trust them."

"You are not far wrong. That is exactly what they will do."

"But...then, let's avoid the city. There is no reason to stir up the controversy all the more."

"We need to go there," says Jess firmly.

"No we don't," insists Pete. "There are many places where you would be welcomed."

"I have told you, Pete, the Son of man *must* suffer many things, even if it means being rejected by the ministers, priests, and rabbis of the

51

opposition. The world's system and my Father's Kingdom are opposed at every turn. The men and women whose minds and hearts are filled with the way the world thinks, they *cannot* understand what I am saying to you. All mankind must eventually see the love of the Father and Son for them. There is no other way to fully demonstrate this love. I have taught you of relinquishment. Now I must show you how to lay down one's life in trust of God. In no other way can the death blow be dealt to your sin than by the willing laying down of life by him who has no sin."

"But surely that cannot be God's will."

"Peter, my dear friend," Jess says earnestly, "after all I have taught you about laying down all but the will of God, you are now speaking from self-will."

"But, Master…it is suicide to continue!"

Jess looks at him, glances slowly around at the rest of us, then back at Peter.

"Get behind me, satan," he says slowly and deliberately.

I am stunned at his words.

Pete retreats a step or two, almost as if being knocked back by the force of the command. His face is white.

Then Jess's voice softens and becomes tender. He steps forward, places a reassuring hand on Pete's shoulder, and gazes into his eyes intently.

"Peter," he says tenderly, "you do not have in mind the things of God but the things of men. When I speak of the world, I do not mean mere wickedness and evil, I speak of looking at things in the way people of the world look at them. The world has become satan's. Its values and attitudes are not my Father's. I am trying to teach you to look at things instead through God's eyes. No one can serve two masters. You must decide which side you are on."

"But why must it be so, Master?" implores Pete, his emotional nature getting the best of him, his eyes filling with tears. "I am afraid for you."

"Because I am the Son of my Father. His will is all."

"And is it His will for—"

He could not complete the question. The same thing was on my mind too.

"It is for me to obey," smiles Jess. "To do His will is my joy, my delight. How else will His people know how to be sons and daughters unless I lead them into an obedience willing to lay down life itself? Do you not yet understand, Peter? My sonship is born in *obedience*."

Again he looks around at the rest of us.

"The relation of the Son to the Father," he goes on, "is the power, the love, the unifying strength by which all of creation hangs together. It is the DNA of the universe. All things emerge out of the bond between the eternal Father and the eternal Son. It is the source of life. Every individual man or woman has the DNA of that relation within him. They are meant to function according to it. The loving power by which the universe was created has been put within each human heart. If one human cell is not in harmony with the divine Fatherhood, it cannot be in harmony with itself. Man is born to sonship, not independent self-rule. Women are born to daughterhood, not to rise high in their own eyes. All are born to childship. It is in order that you may become children that I have been sent to you.

"To become children capable of laying down self-rule is the highest calling, the highest privilege, of humanity. He or she who would grasp for self-rule, who struggles to gain autonomy, who supposes that he has the right to dictate the course of his own steps, and who demands that right in the preservation of independence, will always live alone. But he or she who lays down the claim to self-rule for the higher glory of becoming a child of the Father, he or she steps into the ultimate fellowship of existence—oneness with God the Father, the Creator, the Source of all good, the Fountainhead of happiness and joy, the Heart of eternal life.

"Such is the highest privilege of humanity, yet the most difficult for the independently minded to see. And it is a privilege, a necessity, that must be renewed every successive moment, by the conscious subserving of the will into the higher Will of the Father.

" '*Father, what would You have me to do?*' is the continual prayer of God's children, just as it is my continual prayer every moment. I am my Father's obedient Son. You must become His obedient children.

"These words you hear are not my own, they belong to the Father who sent me. God will honor the one who follows me and heeds my

53

words. I lay down my life by choice. No one takes it from me, but I lay it down of my own accord."

He pauses, then looks around at me. I cannot help but feel the love in his eyes.

"Is this all much different than you expected when you first followed me?" he asks.

I nod.

"Then before we reach the city," he goes on, glancing now at the others of the group, "you should each consider well why you are here, why you followed, and whether you want to continue. It is time again to count the cost. And now you must count it with sobriety and prayer. A party does not lie ahead, but a funeral procession. Do not come unless you know where we are bound. A man who puts his hand to the plough and then looks back is not fit for the Kingdom of God. From this moment on, the price of discipleship will grow, and will become total. Do not deceive yourselves; great opposition is coming."

A heavy silence descends.

"To whom else would we go, Lord," says Pete at length. "You alone have the words of eternal life."

It was the first time any of us had called him *Lord*.

I realized that from now on this is what he was in our lives, what he must be. We are called to be sons and daughters of the Father. He is not only our elder brother...not only our friend...not only our teacher...but our Lord.

Eleven

The Practical Commands

I WAKE EARLY.

Jess is already out. A few of the others are gone too.

I rise and go out. The sun is beginning to come up in the east. I hear voices.

A small group is ahead walking down from a high hill near the place where we had spent the night. Jess is walking in front of them. Light surrounds him. He is bathed in a glow of dazzling white.

He and Pete and John and Jim approach. I sense immediately that there has been a momentous change. Jess's face is radiant. Beside him Pete's face is almost aglow too, as if the light of understanding has at last broken upon him. He looks calmer and more at peace than I have ever seen him. I sense that a transformation has taken place.

I retreat back and do not speak. The moment between the four as they approach seems too holy to intrude upon. They continue toward me. The three with Jess appear awestruck. I follow as they walk back to join the others. Later that morning we continue on our way.

As we near the city, Jess gathers us close around him and begins to teach again. He no longer speaks in obscure teachings that are hard to understand. He becomes very direct and clear.

"What have I been teaching you?" he asks.

"To live in God's Kingdom?" I reply.

"How is that done?"

"By loving God with all your heart," says Pete, "and loving your neighbor as yourself."

"That is correct. You have answered well," replies Jess. "In these two great commandments are summed up all the Law and the Prophets. But now we must clarify what they mean yet more practically. There must be no mistaking what I want you to do. The will of the Father is that you love those He places in your path, that you serve them, are kind to them, and do what good lies in your power to do for them.

"We have been together a long time," he goes on. "But a change is coming and you must be ready for it. Have you been listening to what I have taught? Have they not been very down-to-earth principles? The will of God is no more distant than your neighbor. By seeking the Father's will in obedience to these practicalities will your sonship be perfected.

"Do you seek the will of God? That is why I came, to tell you and show it to you. Such have I been doing all along. Listen and pay attention to what you hear. The Father does not want so much of your worship, your ministry, your emotion, your celebration. He wants your *obedience* in the next moment...and in every moment of your life. So listen to what I tell you.

"I do the will of the Father not because I cannot help it, but because I choose to be an obedient Son. He calls you to that same obedient son-ship, that same obedient daughterhood. I have called you to share in the joy of my obedience."

He pauses and we walk a long way in silence. At length he draws in a deep breath, as if beginning again, and then speaks.

"All right, then," he says. "These are the principles, as simple as I can make them for you to understand, by which you are to demonstrate that you are my Father's children. By these attributes will the world recognize those who belong to my Father. So listen and heed what I am about to tell you.

"God is love," he says. "His essence is love. He sent me to you because He loves the world and every creature in it. I too love all mankind. Therefore, if anyone would be my disciple, he or she must love. That love must be lived out in practicalities not pronouncements; in deeds, not doctrine; in cups of cold water to the thirsty, not pious words of theology. It is the first and highest command of the Kingdom—the ultimate mark of the Father's sons and daughters.

"So this I command you if you would be my disciples. *Love God. Love man.*

"The second of my commands sums up much that I have said to you in a hundred different ways. Find daily opportunities to do good to those around you. Simple goodness holds the world together in the midst of its sin. The constant breaking forth of goodness within and among the world's people is invisible indication that the Kingdom of God is alive in the midst of satan's brief domain. It reminds the world that Someone greater than the prince of darkness is watching over them.

"So this I command you if you would be my disciples. *Be good. Do good.*

"The third great command is to pray. Have you not seen me in constant communion with my Father, before day, at the end of the day, and throughout every day? My spirit is constantly listening to the Father's voice within me. How else can you be one with your heavenly Father unless your heart is open to Him, that He may speak to you, and you to Him. Listen continually to His voice. But remember what I have taught you about prayer—that it must be unseen by those around you. You must make no show of spirituality.

"So this I command you if you would be my disciples. *Pray.*

"Even though goodness blossoms within it, the world does not know my Father. It is a world whose ways are contrary to His ways, whose thoughts are contrary to His thoughts, whose values are contrary to His values. It is a world that will hate you because you belong to me, and will oppose you and ridicule you because of me. It is a world whose prince is the ruler of darkness, satan himself. For as long as you are in the world, therefore, you must be careful and on guard. This enemy will do his utmost to destroy your faith. To walk *in* the world but not *of* the world will require the full power of your heart and mind and soul being focused attentively to the battle between light and darkness of which you are a part. To walk in the light you must perceive the dangers of the darkness.

"So this I command you if you would be my disciples. *Be careful, watchful, alert, and on guard.*

"Because I have called you, and because you have been born into the citizenship of a new Kingdom, henceforth you are no longer citizens of this world. It is not your home. It will be difficult at times not to become lonely and discouraged, for you will be as a pilgrim and foreigner in a strange land. Many hardships, trials, and difficulties will assail you. You will be persecuted, for so have been all God's saints. The life of the disciple requires strength. This is no merry life, frivolous life, easy life, or always a happy life. There is a victory which overcomes the world, but for some that victory lies in the future. I will give you my joy, but it is a joy carved within you by sorrow. Your loyalty, allegiance, and citizenship belong to the Kingdom of God, not the kingdom of man. But do not despair, and fear not, for I have overcome the world. And I will always be with you.

"So this I command you if you would be my disciples. *Take heart. Be courageous. Do not be afraid.*

"In no other way is the love of God so manifest among men as in acts of courtesy and kindness. Gracious and selfless kindness is to characterize your normal mode of behavior toward all you meet. In kindness ought you to carry yourself at all times. Like goodness, the simple virtue of kindness holds the fabric of this present world together in the midst of its sin. Without it, despair would surely reign.

"So this I command you if you would be my disciples. *Treat others with the kindness with which you would have them treat you.*

"It is impossible to be a vigorous citizen of my Father's Kingdom without applying your mind diligently to the principles of that Kingdom. To grow as His sons and daughters will not happen by accident, but only as you carefully learn of the Father's ways, and then energetically obey them. You must keep your mind always awake and alert. When I or my Father speak, it is so that you might learn of our ways, and to help you walk as a son and daughter. You must think with diligence. Otherwise the subtle snares of the world will unknowingly lure you into its values and priorities. You were given minds to use for the glory of God, and to enable you to live powerfully as His sons and daughters.

"So this I command you if you would be my disciples. *Listen carefully. Be clear-minded and mentally diligent. Apply yourselves to learn of and understand the Father's Kingdom.*

"In the world, men rejoice when fate, as they see it, smiles upon them. When things go their way, they are glad. When things go contrary to their wishes, they grumble and complain. But I say to you, when you yield yourselves into the Father's care, nothing occurs outside His design. Therefore, complaint is no longer to have any part in your life. Thank God for everything. For if you allow it, He will make good come of it.

"So this I command you if you would be my disciples. *Rejoice whatever your circumstances.*

"As my followers, you are called to a new and distinctive standard in your relationships than is practiced by the world. You have heard that it was said, 'Love your neighbor and hate your enemy.' But I say to you, love *all* men, and make the most strenuous effort toward those whom the world would say you are not obligated to care about. Your love of these will set you apart as belonging to the Father's family.

"So this I command you if you would be my disciples. *Do good, pray for, and forgive those who do you wrong.*

"The words of your mouth are constant indication of the attitudes that lie deep in your heart. Therefore, guard your tongue, say what you mean, and let your words be seasoned with salt in all circumstances and about all people.

"So this I command you if you would be my disciples. *Speak with grace.*

"As I have served you, so must you serve one another.

"So this I command you if you would be my disciples. *Be a servant.*

"It is impossible to be a child, in the childlikeness of the Kingdom, while self-will rules. All motives must be abandoned into the will of God. Especially must your supposed rights be abandoned, that most subtle stumbling block of pride with which the world is so infected. Beware, it will seek to delude you at every turn. Lay it down.

"So this I command you if you would be my disciples. *Deny yourself. Lose your life in the will of the Father.*

"The harmony of brotherhood, the peace of compassionate affection, is to characterize your relationships with others of your kind. In the world there is strife between men and women, each seeking his and her own good at the expense of their neighbor. It shall not be so among you. Whoever would be first among you must be last of all and servant of all. I want you to walk in peace and harmony, esteeming others ahead of yourself.

"So this I command you if you would be my disciples. *Be devoted to, reconciled, united, and at peace with all men.*

"The self-righteous man or woman, proud of his or her accomplishments, proud of his standing, and especially those proud of their spirituality, can have no part in the Kingdom of God. Pride was satan's downfall and is the very air by which his temporary rule on earth is sustained— everyone thinking more highly of themselves than they were created to think. He who would walk with my Father must breathe a different air, the air of submission. Humility is the oxygen of the Kingdom.

"So this I command you if you would be my disciples. *Do not exalt yourself. Walk in meekness and humility.*

"Once you have given yourself to the Father, your life is no longer your own. Its cares are not yours, its worries are not yours. You are in His hands now, just as I have been during this sojourn of mine among you. You may believe in His goodness. He is a good Father who will accomplish good in your life. You may trust Him in all things.

"So this I command you if you would be my disciples. *Do not worry. Trust God. Have faith. Believe.*

"As my Father's sons and daughters, you are called to an extraordinary life, visibly distinct from the world. You are to be different than other men and women, not by external appearances, but in character, motive, and attitude—better in all ways. You are to reflect the nature and character and goodness of your Father in Heaven.

"So this I command you if you would be my disciples. *Be righteous.*

"How else will the world see love in you unless your compassion is visible and active? Therefore, do good. Let your light shine with deeds before men. Care for the needy. Give cups of cold water to the thirsty and dying. Let your hands be the Father's hands among the less fortunate.

Otherwise, you will have no part in me and it will be as if I never knew you.

"So this I command you if you would be my disciples. *Care for those in need. Give to the poor.*

"The rewards of childship are not immediate, as many teach who do not know my Father's ways. Believe me when I assure you that all who have left home or land or family or wealth for the Kingdom will receive a hundred times more in the life to come. For many who are first will be last, and the last first. But much in this present life will be hard, and those rewards from my Father's hand are often not easily visible. You will not always have wealth, health, or happiness. If you ask Him for bread, He will not give you a stone. But to the unseeing it may appear a stone. Your life may appear hard and its blessings may not be visible. Therefore, hold fast to what I have taught you, and cling to your Father's hand. His true children will be given a crown of righteousness on that day.

"So this I command you if you would be my disciples. *Persevere and endure in faith.*"

The discussion and our many questions regarding the practical list of commands he is giving us lasts two days. Occasionally one or another of our number starts to write down what he is saying. An IRS auditor named Matt is one of the most persistent. But each time, Jess stops him and makes him put his writing things away.

"The time for remembering will come," he says. "When it does, the Holy Spirit will bring everything back into your minds. For now I do not want you to categorize my teaching. It too easily becomes mere theology, and turns hard and inflexible. These commands contain the power to transform you into the Father's sons and daughters. Do not remove that power by trying to systematize them. I want you to see, through these things I am telling you, what kind of man and woman is my follower. I do not want you to memorize them. I want you to be the kind of person characterized by these priorities, who *lives* these qualities, and thus brings glory to your Father in Heaven.

"Do not learn a list such as, *I must pray, I must be kind, I must not worry,* so that you can analyze it. Instead, pray, be kind, and trust your Father. I came that you might become sons and daughters of your Father.

"Do not *study* every attribute of sonship. There is no power in the studying of them. There is only power in *doing* them. The power in the commands I give you is the power to transform you from selfish and prideful men and women into self-denying sons and daughters of the Most High.

"Do not dogmatize my teaching. Be His children."

Twelve

The Evidence of Love

WE COME TO THE CITY.

As we suspect, the opposition has grown powerful since we left for the country in the north. As we approach, many recognize us and huge crowds flock to greet us. Even before we get there, word has gone before us, such that as we enter the city it is like nothing we have yet seen. Singing and shouting all accompany us, people calling *"Hallelujah," "Praise the Lord," "Hosanna,"* and *"Blessed is the Lord,"* as we go by.

Jess remains calm. The acclaim of the crowd does not move him. Indeed, by the next day the opposition begins again to test him with their tricks and questions, trying to turn the people against him.

After a few days of this, I sense again, as I have many times recently, a yet deeper quiet coming to his spirit. He takes us aside one evening to enjoy a supper alone together at the house of one of his followers in the city, a wealthy widow named Mary, who lives with her brother Barny and her enthusiastic young son Mark.

The mood is subdued. He reminds us of our discussions of the last several days. As we prepare to eat the meal, he gets up and takes a basin of water and a towel.

"Take off your shoes," he says.

Puzzled, we all do so.

Jess then proceeds to wash our feet one at a time, though at first Pete objects. None of us says a word throughout the proceeding. Of course it

63

feels good and refreshing, for the day has been long. But it is strange for *him* to wash *our* feet.

When he is through, he dries his hands with the towel and resumes his seat.

"Do you understand what I have just done?" he asks.

We remain silent. Everything is always so unexpected with him. We never know what to say to his probing questions.

"You call me Teacher and Lord," he goes on, "and rightly so, for that is what I am. So if I, your Lord and Teacher, have washed your feet, should you not also wash each other's feet? You see, in everything, as in this instance, I have been setting an example that I want you to follow. It is my desire that you do what I do. You will be greatly blessed if you do so."

"Do you want us to wash each other's feet...*now*?" asks Pete, eager to obey, yet uncertain of his meaning.

Jess smiles. "No, Pete," he says. "Once you are clean you have no need to wash again. I have done this to help you see that in the Kingdom of God, everything is upside-down from the kingdom of man. In the world, greatness would lord it over others. But in God's Kingdom the only greatness is to serve. As I have just shown you, to be great means washing the feet of your brothers and sisters. The Son of Man came to serve, and to give His life as a ransom for many."

He grows quiet, then looks to our treasurer, a man named Judd.

"What you must do, Judd," he says, "do quickly."

Puzzled, we watch as the man called Judd Simonson rises from the table, a strange look in his eyes, and leaves the room. By now it is late and dark, for it is night.

When he is gone, Jess glances around the table.

"Do you love me?" he asks.

Pete blurts out an answer.

"Lord, how can you ask such a thing?" he says. "You know that we do."

"If you love me, then," Jess continues, "you will keep the commandments I have given you. This is the only way to be my followers, by doing what I say."

"What is chief among them?" asks Tad.

"A new commandment I give to you," replies Jess. "It is what I have been teaching you from the beginning: Love one another. As I have loved you, so you must love one another. This is how others will know that you are my disciples—not because you tell them of me, not because you convince them that my teaching is true, not because you work miracles before their very eyes, not even because you tell them about our God and Father in Heaven. None of these will cause people to believe, but only if you love one another. Your love is the *only* way they can come to know the truth. Your words will matter nothing, your deeds will matter everything."

"But, Lord, why are you speaking like this?" says Pete.

"Do not let your hearts be troubled," says Jess, sensing his anxiety. "Trust in God. Trust also in me. Where I am going, you cannot follow now, but you will follow later. And you know the way to where I am going."

"Lord, we don't know where you are going," says Tom. "So how can we know the way?"

"I am the way and the truth and the life. I have come to take you to the Father. When you really know me, you will know my Father as well. From now on, you do know Him, because you have seen Him."

"Show us the Father," says Phil, "and that will be enough."

"Do you not know me yet, Phil, even after I have been with you so long? Don't you believe that I am in the Father and the Father in me? God and I are one. I do not speak of my own accord, but the Father who sent me commanded me what to say and how to say it. God loves you because you have loved me and have believed that I came from Him. I came from the Father and entered the world. Now I am leaving the world and going back to the Father."

Jess pauses and gazes intently toward Phil.

"Anyone who has seen me has seen the Father," he says. "As the Father has loved me, so have I loved you. I have called you my friends, for everything that I learned from my Father I have made known to you."

"But...but it sounds like you are leaving us soon," I say, "—very soon."

"I must leave you," he replies. "All must be fulfilled. But I will ask the Father, and He will give you another, a Helper and Guide and Friend to be with you forever, the Spirit of Truth, the Holy Spirit, God's own Spirit. He will come to you, and will lead you into all truth."

"But what are we to do when you are gone?" asks Bart.

"You are to do as I have taught you," answers Jess. "Whoever has my commands and obeys them, he it is who loves me. If you love me, you will obey my teaching, My Father will love you and we will come and make our home with you. The words that I have spoken are not my own. They are the words of the Father, who lives in me. Peace I leave with you, my peace I give you. Do not let your hearts be troubled, and do not be afraid."

"How can we possibly live without you?" says John. He is younger than all the rest and Jess has always loved him with a special tenderness. Tears now fill his eyes.

"I am the vine and you are the branches," says Jess. "My Father is the gardener. If you abide in me and allow me to abide in you, you will bear much fruit. That is how you will live when I am gone. But apart from me you can do nothing. As the Father has loved me, so have I loved you. Now abide in my love. If you obey my commands you will abide in my love, just as I have obeyed my Father's commands and abide in His love. I have told you all this so that my joy may be in you and that your joy may be complete.

"My command is this: Love one another as I have loved you. Greater love has no one than he who lays down his life for his friends. You are my friends if you do as I have commanded you. Everything that I learned from my Father I have made known to you. This is my command: Love one another.

"There is much more that I have to teach you. But our time now is short. When the Spirit of truth comes, He will guide you into all truth. Now come, it is time for us to go."

Jess rises, and we follow.

Thirteen

Garden of Relinquishment

W E WALK OUT INTO THE CITY, WHICH IS NOW QUIET AND PEACEFUL in the evening air. We gather closely, for Jess is subdued and speaking quietly.

We approach a favorite spot, the expansive park just outside the city where I had earlier followed as he talked with Nick.

It is late and most are sleepy.

"Sit here," says Jess, "while I go pray." His voice is heavy and disconsolate. "I must seek God's will."

The night in the park grows late. Some of our number gradually fall asleep.

I am restless. I rise and begin to walk about.

Not wanting to intrude upon the Master's private communion in prayer, I am yet irresistibility drawn toward the voice I hear faintly through the darkness. On tiptoe I approach closer through the trees, then ·stop. His words of prayer are more pained and full of heartache than I have ever heard from him. I know he is weeping as he pours his heart out to God.

"...that I might glorify You..." I hear him say, "that they may know You, the only true God...whom You have sent...I pray for them, Father...protect them...so that they may be one as we are one..."

As I listen, the incredible truth strikes me that he is praying for us!

I inch a few steps closer.

"...that they may have the full measure of my joy within them...sanctify them by the truth...Your Word is truth..."

It falls silent for some time. I wait. Gradually I hear him praying again.

"...not for them alone...all those who will believe...that they may be one as we are one...may they be brought to complete unity...that the world may know that You sent me...that the love You have for me may be in them and that I myself may be in them."

Again it is silent. After some moments, suddenly a cry of anguish bursts from the Lord's mouth.

"I know what is coming!" he cries. "I cannot bear the thought of it. Please, Father, if it be possible, if there is any other way, let this agony pass from me!"

A momentary pause comes. The night is silent. Not a breath of air disturbs the stillness.

Then I hear in a trembling voice, barely audible—

"Nevertheless, not my will, but Yours be done."

The words are followed by quiet weeping. No other sounds come from the depths of the park.

I sit down on the ground and now grow sleepy myself. Soon, without realizing it, I doze off.

Sometime later a sound wakes me. I glance up with a start. It is him, returning from the depths of the park. His eyes are red and moist with tears. He nods in greeting as I rise.

"You have been a faithful follower, my friend," he says with a thin smile. "Remember what I said earlier—be watchful, vigilant, but fear not."

He places a hand on my shoulder and gazes yet more intently into my eyes.

"A great trial is coming to you all," he says. "You must pray diligently to be strong and not fall into temptation. Stand firm in your faith. Trust God. He will bring great victory from it, even unto the salvation of the world."

I nod, but do not understand. I follow him as the others gradually wake. In the distance I hear voices approaching through the night.

Fourteen

Accusation and Denial

A BAND OF MEN IS COMING ALONG THE PATH THROUGH THE GARDEN carrying lanterns and lights and, I think, a few weapons of some kind. There appear to be 30 or 40 in number and they are obviously agitated. In front walk the men I recognize as leaders in the protest movement. Behind them an ugly crowd strings along, many of whom it is obvious have been drinking.

We are immediately filled with fear and begin to run out of the park. Everyone scatters in twos and threes. I see Pete, Andy, Nate, Jim, Phil, Tad, Bart, and Matt all disappearing in the night.

I sprint after them, finding a place to hide and watch in the trees.

Jess steps forward as the band approaches. The chief evangelist, flanked on each side by the cardinal and rabbi, walk toward him then stop. They are followed by a few dozen powerful and well-known pastors, speakers, elders, worship leaders, bishops, musicians, deacons, scribes, priests, authors, and Pharisees.

"Who is it you want?" Jess asks calmly.

"Jess Josephson," says Dr. Caphas, the evangelist.

"I am he."

Not expecting him to be so direct, or to not make an attempt to escape, no one replies immediately.

"Am I the leader of a rebellion," Jess says looking around at them, "that you must come to me like this, in the dead of night with a mob behind you? Have I not been in the middle of the city among you every day? But this is your hour, when darkness reigns, so let the Scriptures be fulfilled."

"We have had enough of all that, Josephson," says Caphas. "I assume you know who we are."

"I do."

"We are extremely influential leaders in our religious communities. The people listen to us and do what we say. We have put up with this nonsense you have been preaching long enough. We have come to demand that you stop. But we are reasonable men. We know that many of your followers are sincere people. Some of your teaching, even, is acceptable according to our doctrinal guidelines. So we are prepared to offer you a deal."

I am hiding amid some trees listening, incredulous that they would dare speak to him like this.

"Our deal," continues Caphas, "is in the form of a compromise. We are prepared to offer certain concessions, give you a position of some importance, perhaps, in the church or synagogue of your choice...*if* you will join us rather than continuing to undermine us. In that light then, I have just a few simple questions to ask you."

He pauses to adjust his tie, then assumes a dignified posture.

"We have witnesses that claim you said you would destroy the church and rebuild it in three days," he says. "Is this charge true?"

Jess does not reply.

"Answer him!" shouts someone from behind. A big rough man steps forward and strikes Jess a full blow across the face, nearly knocking him to the ground. A gash from the side of his mouth begins to bleed freely.

I wince in shock. How could this be happening to such a kind and gentle man!

Suddenly a voice speaks right beside me!

"Hey, you're one of them!"

I leap at the sound and spin around. I thought no one could see me here.

"No...no, you're mistaken," I falter. "I...I'm just watching, that's all."

"I saw you with him yesterday," the man insists. "You were beside him when they were arguing about who will be in Heaven. Hey!" he shouts toward the scene in the clearing, "Hey…I've got another one of the ringleaders over here!"

"You're crazy!" I cry in terror, starting to back away. "I don't know what you're talking about. I don't know the man!"

At last I find my feet in earnest and dash off. Behind me I hear the evangelist's voice booming out in anger.

"I charge you under oath to tell me if you are the Son of God," yells Dr. Caphas.

"It is as you say," replies Jess. "And I tell you that you will see the Son of Man…"

"We need hear no more," interrupts the cardinal. "This is blasphemy pure and simple!"

Dr. Caphas draws close to Jess.

"Look," he says, "be reasonable. If you don't accept our deal and deny this absurd claim about being the Son of God, we cannot be responsible for what may happen. This mob is in a violent mood. You can see that as well as I. There are those—I've heard rumors—who are likely to be less lenient than we are. I have heard some call for your imprisonment, even death. We are your only hope. There are forces at work which we may not be able to stop if this goes on too long. Do you understand, we may not be able to protect you?"

"If I have spoken falsely," says Jess, "then tell me plainly."

"You are an imbecile!" shouts Caphas, throwing his hands up in the air and glancing around at his colleagues. "I am telling you that your life is in danger, and you insist on playing your games with words like you've been doing all week."

He shakes his head in irritated exasperation. "Take him away," he says. "I am through with him!"

He turns as the crowd grabs Jess, ties his hands, and leads him out of the park and back toward the city.

Fifteen

Despair

I SLOW IN MY FLIGHT. NO ONE IS CHASING ME NOW.

I pause and glance around. I hear the crowd returning to the city. Lights and voices recede in the distance. When all is quiet, I steal out from cover and follow.

They take Jess to a holding cell where they convince the man on duty to lock him up until morning.

The rest of the night passes like a horrible nightmare. I fear I am being watched and followed.

Someone comes up to me as I run through the street.

"I recognize you," she says, pointing to me. "You were with him. You are part of that gang."

"No," I shout again. A curse erupts from my lips. "I don't know who you are talking about!"

I run off, tears stinging my eyes for my cowardice.

I do not sleep all night, but wander aimlessly. When morning comes, a great crowd gathers outside the jail where he is being held. The protest leaders arrive to take Jess, still bound, to the county magistrate, Judge Pilar. I follow in the midst of the crowd. I see most of the others of our number, including the women and Jess's mother, scattered among the throng as it surges along.

Hearing the commotion from the mob as they approach, the judge comes out onto the balcony of the large main courthouse building. Dr. Caphas steps to the front of the huge mob.

"We have brought this man to you," he calls up to the judge. "He has been subverting our nation."

"In what way?" asks Judge Pilar.

"He tells the people not to pay taxes."

"A serious charge...but this is a free country. It is not against the law to say such things."

"He claims to be a king."

"He hardly looks like a king to me!" laughs the judge. "I hardly think the nation is in danger."

"All right then, he claims to be the Son of God."

"What!" laughs Pilar. "Is this nothing but a religious dispute? Haven't you heard of separation of church and state?"

He turns and begins to walk back inside.

"Wait," calls Caphas. "This is different."

"This is no civil matter," rejoins Pilar, "—why have you brought him to me?"

"He is dangerous, a rabble-rouser," insists Caphas.

"What is that to me?" replies the judge. "My hands are clean in the affair. I find no basis for a legal charge against the man. Deal with him yourself."

Pilar turns and walks back inside.

Thwarted, the leading pastors and priests begin to stir up the crowd. Shouts and threats sound from all about. Yelling and commotion quickly get out of hand. More and more people step forward to strike him.

"The man who would be a king...look at him now!"

The crowd is ugly and menacing.

Suddenly Pete runs forward from somewhere, a large knife in his hand.

"Get away...stand back everyone!" he cries, swinging the knife about wildly. One look in his eyes makes it clear that he is ready to kill or be killed to free Jess from the mob.

The crowd around him pulls back.

"Okay, Caphas, the rest of you," shouts Pete. "Release him!"

But now Jess steps calmly toward his friend.

"Pete," he says, "put it away. This is not God's way."

In the midst of the hysteria, Judd appears from out of nowhere. We have not seen him since he left the supper we had eaten together last night.

The leaders seem to know him. We see a few nods being exchanged. Fearing his own arrest, Pete now sheaths his knife and disappears again into the mass of humanity.

Judd walks straight toward Jess.

"Hello, Teacher," he says, then steps forward and kisses him on the cheek.

"Judd, my friend," says Jess, sadly shaking his head. "I am so sorry. But my love for you is unchanged. Now, do what you came for."

Judd steps back, his face white from the words he has just heard. It suddenly seems to dawn on him that he has made a terrible mistake. But it is too late.

We hear shouts.

"Look out...get back!"

A man emerges from the crowd into the opening made by Judd's approach. He has a gun!

"Back everyone...a terrorist!" screams a woman's voice.

"Run for your lives...it's an automatic!"

In a frenzy the crowd flees.

Suddenly shots explode in the morning air. Hysteria breaks out. Men, women, and children flee in panic, trampling about, knocking each other down, yelling and scurrying madly, expecting any second to hear the terrifying sound of machine gun fire spraying the crowd. I am jostled about and nearly knocked to the ground.

It only takes a few seconds for those nearby to clear away. I regain my balance and hurriedly glance toward where Jess was standing a moment ago.

There, at the center of the pandemonium, the man of peace lies in a pool of his own blood.

Sixteen

Ultimate Sonship

MORTIFIED AT WHAT I HAVE DONE TO THIS ONE WHO HAS GIVEN SO MUCH, who has given me life itself—denying him when he needed me most, following from a distance, pretending not even to know him—I approach the gruesome scene.

The crowd is scattering in all directions. The hired gunman has disappeared. Within minutes most of the terrified spectators are gone.

Neither Dr. Caphas nor any of the other leaders of the protest movement are to be seen anywhere. Judd too has disappeared.

It is about noon.

On the ground where he lays dying, Jess is in obvious agony. I faintly hear him whisper, "Father, forgive them, for they do not know what they have done."

Sensing my approach, he looks up with heavy eyelids and smiles. The love in his eyes says all, and I know he forgives me. I stoop down beside him.

"Do you see what all this means?" he says softly.

All I can do is shake my head weeping freely.

"To live out my obedient sonship," he says, "and to give you the example of obedience...that you too might live."

"But you are dying!" I cry. My heart is breaking. "Why would the Father want you to die?"

"For your sake," he answers.

"My sake! How can that be? I denied you! I do not deserve your love, still less your forgiveness!"

I break down, sobbing in anguish.

"Of course you do not deserve it," he says softly. "But I love you just the same. And my Father loves you and forgives you too. Do not forget, He sent me to you because of His great love."

"But it seems senseless," I wail, "for you to die like this."

"To you at this moment, perhaps. But out of my death will come the power to defeat death altogether, and bring eternal life to all the world."

"But how can such a thing be?"

"It is the Father's way," smiles Jess. "Remember what I taught you, His Kingdom is upside-down from the world's. Things work differently in His economy. Trust our Father to accomplish His victory of salvation and reconciliation."

He smiles up at me, then struggles to lift his hand. He takes mine in his for a moment. I can feel the strength ebbing out of this body that was once so strong.

"Ah, little one," he says, "in dying to self...in the self-willing abandonment into the Father's will is life. I am only dying to my flesh. But out of such death will eternal life be born."

He finds my eyes, and again probes deeply, as he has on two important occasions before.

"Are you willing to die with me?" he asks.

I stare into his eyes. But before I answer, a few more of his followers slowly come forward. Pete stoops down at my side, Andy next to him, then Jim, John, Bart, Phil, Tom, and the others. I am no longer afraid for what will happen to me. It doesn't seem to matter now.

We are all weeping. Jess looks around and speaks a few personal words to each one in turn.

Behind us another figure approaches. We rise to give her room. It is his mother.

Mary kneels beside him. She takes his hand as they exchange a few words. We wait patiently for perhaps three or four minutes, not hearing what they say. At last she bends forward, kisses his cheek, then leans back, tears flowing freely down her face.

As we cluster around him, Jess lays on the ground. Occasionally he speaks, but his body is weakening. He seems at peace. The women weep. An hour goes by, then two.

Passersby approach from time to time and jeer. A few taunt and make fun of him. But generally a quietness hovers over the place, a mood of waiting for the inevitable. Even the officials and police officers who have been sent to keep order seem moved by the solemnity of the occasion.

About two-thirty, he seems struggling to speak.

"I...I am thirsty," he says.

Two drifters are walking by drinking. Both look like criminals.

"Here, you so-called king!" says one of them. He walks over and pours some of the cheap wine from the bottle he is holding over Jess's face, then laughs crudely. "Why don't you save yourself if you're a king!" he yells down mockingly.

"What right have you to taunt him?" says the other as they begin to walk away. "Do you have no respect? If you and I got shot, it would be no more than we deserve. But this man has done nothing wrong."

He pauses, then glances back.

"Remember me," he says down to Jess.

Jess struggles to reassure him with a faint smile and nod.

Gradually clouds move overhead. The sky darkens.

Suddenly about three o'clock, Jess cries out loudly in anguish.

"Oh, Father," bursts from his lips. "I...I commend my spirit... Father—it is finished!"

I look down. His eyes are closed. I know he is gone.

The next instant the sky erupts with a brilliant flash of light, followed by a crash of thunder.

A few officials come forward, confer briefly with his mother, then pick up the body, and carry it to a funeral home.

Seventeen

A Yet Greater Shock

I FOLLOW THE SILENT PROCESSION TO THE FUNERAL PARLOR belonging to a family friend named Joe who has offered its use without charge.

Jess's body is laid to rest in a small room awaiting funeral plans. As it is the weekend and his death such a sudden shock, nothing is done other than place it in a cooler, which is closed, then the door to the place locked.

Disconsolate, I stumble away alone. The hours pass, I hardly remember how. Everyone has scattered. I do not even know where the others are. Some, I think, are staying at Mary and Barny's house. Rumors are circulating that others of us could be arrested. But I am not so much afraid as in shock. I don't know what to do, what to think.

Night arrives, and with it the sleepless agony of guilt and despair. Morning brings no relief. Another long day of misery follows. I see a few of our comrades coming and going in and out of the houses of friends. We share furtive glances but are afraid to acknowledge one another openly.

Another night. Sleep still contains no relief from the torment. Now the accusations are being hurled at me from within my own conscience.

"You denied him...you are a coward," come the tormenting voices. "You lied to save your own skin. He loved you. And you repaid it by turning your back on him. You didn't stand up to help him or protect him. You might as well have pulled the trigger yourself."

What little rest comes and goes is fitful and tormented. I have hardly slept in three days. My body is exhausted, my brain scorched into numbness.

81

Again I wake. Another morning arrives, but it brings only reminders…and a deepening of the waking nightmare that life has become.

The sun is shining.

I go out. The morning is quiet. Unconsciously I find myself drawn in the direction of the funeral home. Perhaps, I think, there will be some news by now regarding the funeral.

Suddenly the ground convulses beneath me. An earthquake! It rumbles and quivers for five or ten seconds, then gradually calms.

A little shaken, I continue on.

I draw close to the funeral home. Ahead I see three women running toward me. As they approach I recognize two of the Marys and Joanna. I pause, thinking perhaps they are running from some danger caused by the earthquake and need help.

But the expressions on their faces are of wonder and joy. They are shouting and waving, but I can scarcely make out a word.

Before I have a chance to find out, I hear footsteps running from behind. I turn to see young John sprinting along the street toward me.

Now come more people running. Everyone is shouting, filling the quiet morning with questions.

What is wrong? Is a mass arrest underway? Are they rounding us all up…is everyone trying to escape while they can?

"Is it true…is it true?" shouts John.

"Yes…yes, John!" Joanna yells back excitedly. "Where are Pete and Jim?"

"Behind me," answers John. "They're coming."

He dashes off in the direction of the funeral home. The women also hurry away. Bewildered, I begin to follow John. Soon I hear running steps behind me again.

Once more I turn. This time it is Pete and Jim, both running hard but obviously tired.

I pause to wait for them.

"What is it…what's happening?" I ask as Pete runs up.

"Haven't you heard?" he says.

"No...heard what?"

"They say the Lord is alive."

"Alive!" I exclaim.

"An angel appeared to some of the women," says Pete. "He told them he has risen."

"But...he was dead!"

"I know. I didn't believe it myself at first either. But Mary has actually seen him."

"She's seen him?"

"And talked to him. Yes, it's true...he's alive—really alive!"

Eighteen

Feed My Sheep

THE ASTONISHING NEWS IS TRUE!

Jess is alive, come back to life from the dead! The resurrection is an unbelievable, life-changing reality!

We find the funeral home empty. The bloodstained blanket still lay spread on the table where they had placed him, but there is no body where Jess had been two days before.

Suddenly begins to return to my mind so much he had said. I remember that he had told us he would die and rise again. But I was too dense and dull to grasp his meaning. No wonder he was always talking about eternal life conquering death!

He appears to us all that same evening when we are together eating supper. We see him and speak to him and great is our rejoicing. It happens that Tom isn't with us at the time and doesn't believe it when we tell him about it. But a week later he appears to us again. This time the Lord makes Tom put his finger in the bullet hole in his chest.

The next few weeks are glorious and happy.

The Lord appears to us many more times, and teaches us many new things he wants us to know now that we understand the truth of his resurrection. I did not understand him when he spoke figuratively. Neither could I understand him when he spoke plainly. But now all at once so much begins to make new sense. Some of what he has to say now is even more difficult. Yet almost as if by a miracle, I feel as if my heart and mind have been suddenly unlocked and I understand everything, just as he said we would.

"Rejoice not in the suffering I endured for your sake," he says, "but in my obedience. Then take my example, my very life, into your own. To bring you this life of self-denying relinquishment is why I came, and why I called you to follow me."

"Must...we too...must we die?" I ask.

"Of course," he replies. "It is the only path to your sonship...the death of empty-handed obedience, the empty hands of faith."

"When will I die?" I ask.

"You must die every day," he says with a smile. "Every moment when you lift the empty hands of faith to the Father is its own tiny death, death to your own motives, making you alive to the Father's will and purpose. To obey is to slay the self. To say, *Not my will, but Yours,*" is to close the eternal link between God's Fatherhood and your sonship. I am not the Son of God because I cannot help it. I was not sent among you as an angel, but as a man with free will, just like you. I have chosen my Sonship by closing that eternal circle between myself and the Father, just as you must do every day."

After he returns to life, he comes and goes and is not always with us. Some return to their homes and jobs. Though our hearts are full of joy, we don't know what we are supposed to do.

One day, back at the coastal town where several of the men live and where I had been staying when I first saw Jess, I am out in Pete's fishing boat with Pete, Tom, Jim, Tad, John, and Andy. We have been working all night but have caught nothing. The recent storms have stirred up the waters.

In the morning as we troll along near the shore, we see a man standing on the beach beside a fire.

"Have you any fish?" he calls out to us across the water.

"No, nothing," Pete calls back. "Not much of a night."

"Try the other side of your boat," the man calls back.

Puzzled by the strange advice, Pete turns to us, then shrugs his shoulders as if to say, "What do we have to lose?"

So we try it. Within minutes the fish are practically jumping up into the boat. We soon have a catch of more than a hundred!

In the midst of our sudden activity, John glances at the man beside the fire. Suddenly recognition dawns over his face.

"It is the Lord!" he cries.

Pete turns. Overjoyed, he jumps into the water and swims ashore.

The rest of us follow in the boat, and haul it onto the beach. As I walk up I can smell fish cooking on the open fire.

"Come and have some breakfast," says Jess.

We sit down and warm ourselves while he serves us the fish with some fresh bread.

When we have finished, Jess speaks to Pete.

"Peter Johnson," he says, "do you love me?"

"Yes, Lord," replies Pete, "you know that I do."

"Feed my lambs," he says.

He glances around to the rest of us.

"Do you also love me?" he asks.

I nod. A few answer as Pete had.

"Then feed my sheep."

I quietly ponder his words.

Still a third time he asks the same question.

"Do you love me?"

And yet again Pete and the rest of us assure him that we do.

"Then feed my sheep," he says again.

Slowly Jess rises. Pete follows him along the beach. Somehow the rest of us realize that this is a private moment meant for Pete alone, although John also rises and follows from a distance.

Nineteen

Reality Becomes Reality

As I WATCH, GRADUALLY THE SCENE BEFORE ME BEGINS TO CHANGE. Listening to the powerful exchange beside the fire and following Pete and Jess with my eyes as they move away from me, slowly their voices grow softer.

I rise and find myself walking slowly, backward from the fire. The smoke and pleasing aroma of roasted fish grows faint in my nostrils.

Slowly I continue, unconscious of movement, not actually feeling the motion of my legs beneath me, yet observing the shoreline and the figures of my friends recede from me.

Now I am moving over the path up over the rise of sand, then along the path through the beach grasses that cover the low dunes.

I continue to watch, but from a greater and greater distance. Jess and Pete grow smaller and smaller in the distance. They continue to talk, but no longer can I hear them. John is still following.

The voices of my other friends around the fire also grow soft. Then the images of their forms fade and become indistinct...

Gradually, as if coming out of a waking daydream, I become aware of myself as I sit at the window looking out upon the stormy northwest Pacific. I realize that I am staring at several people I do not know in the distance walking along the water's edge about two hundred yards away. Perhaps, for all I can tell, one of them may be a local fisherman, for the seas are still rough, and the nearby fleet of boats is safely battened down in the harbor.

Two or three people are sitting around a small beach fire that I still faintly smell as it blows in my direction.

Realizing what has happened, and that I have just emerged from a life-changing vision of Christ's ever–present reality, I slowly slip to my knees.

> *Oh, Lord Jesus, I whisper. I thank You for Your reality in my life. I thank You for drawing me by Your Spirit into the events by which You won our salvation through Your obedient Sonship. Thank You for finding me in the midst of the crowd and calling me to follow You. Thank You for probing ever deeper into my heart so that I would be confronted with the reality of who You truly are, the Son of the Father, the Son of God. Thank You for what that revelation means in the lives of all…and in my own life most of all.*
>
> *Thank You for the commands by which You continually pressed Your disciples to live in God's Kingdom amid realities close by them, and among the people near them every day. Let me heed that teaching and that example. Help me live my discipleship immediately… now…in the next five minutes…as I look into the eyes of the next person You send across the path of my life. Help me think and behave toward him or her as You would were You walking in my world right now.*
>
> *Thank You for showing us the Father, whom You came to reveal. And thank You for dying for me, that I might know and experience in my own life the power of relinquishment, and the daily reality of obedient sonship. Help me to be an obedient son of Your Father and mine.*

I rise and return to my paper and pen. My mind and heart are full of many new thoughts about this man Jesus Christ, the Son of God.

PART 2

I Want You

Twenty

To What Does Jesus Call Us?

WERE YOU ABLE TO PUT YOURSELF IN THE PICTURE AS I DID, envisioning Jesus suddenly turning the world upside down where you live—be it office, factory, retirement home, school, store, small town, suburban neighborhood, city business district—with your being swept up in it too, like I was?

How can we not follow Him, you and I? Who wouldn't want to run along to see what it is all about?

Why did I go after that crowd outside the window of my mind's eye?

Because I am not one who believes that Jesus is to be kept in stained glass windows and old-fashioned paintings and stuffy quiet churches— no, not even in upbeat contemporary churches. He is no Christ contained within four walls...any kind of walls. If His life has meaning, then His example must be brought into life with us, and we taken into His life with Him.

The life of Jesus has no more significance than any other historical figure unless we learn to walk beside Him, and bring Him alongside us where we live and among those we see every day. Not in a white robe and sandals and speaking King James English, but as a *real* man, a *real* friend, a *real* Son of God...a *real* Lord.

As one who says, "If you would be My follower, forgive *that* man— not some impersonal 'man' in the Bible, but that man you are with every day who treats you so rudely. Find something kind to do for *that* woman—the one whom you don't like and who grates on you so. Do not

93

reply to that charge against you by the lady in your church but walk in humility. Take the beam out of your own eye in relation to that man whose fault is so glaring in your eyes. Place that irritating person's welfare ahead of your own. Pay more attention to what I say. You are thinking in the world's way. Trust God. Rejoice. Do as you would be done by."

We're just fooling ourselves if we pretend to be His followers, but all the while keep the gutsy commands that came from His mouth at arm's length, where we quote them in somber tones but don't do them.

It's become too easy in our day to hide behind, "Jesus lives in my heart," when there is no such standard indicating discipleship in the Gospels. The only standard is the one the Lord Himself set: If you love Me, you will keep My commands.

If anything can be said about the disciples' life with Jesus, it is that He never let them hide behind comfortable jargon. He was constantly throwing them curves, saying the most outrageous things, laying on the most disconcerting requirements and not allowing them to squirm out of what He said.

Think of the person you loathe most in the world, or have the most difficult relationship with, preferably someone who has treated you detestably and spoken against you, perhaps even told lies about you or spread false rumors about you. Then imagine yourself going to that person—*today*...right now, before you read the rest of this book—and doing some genuinely kind and gracious thing for them, with a heart of love and forgiveness, with no vibes or hint of attitude, especially with no pride in yourself for being so spiritual...truly *giving* yourself to serve that man or woman in meekness and humility, without a word of thanks, per-haps walking away at the end with said person laughing behind your back and thinking you a bigger sap than ever.

That's a tough assignment. There are some people in my life like that. I don't relish the idea of what I've suggested one bit.

But picture something akin to that in your mind's eye—make it more difficult, more crucifying to your flesh and your pride if you can—and you've begun to get a faint glimmer of the kind of life to which Jesus called His followers.

And living like that all day...every day.

94

Literally...putting *others* first, in all circumstances, in all situations. Doing as you would be done by.

Men and women, my friends, He calls us to be *servants*...slaves. Nothing more, nothing less.

That's the kind of sonship and daughterhood He came to example for us.

Going to church six times a week doesn't make you a follower of Christ. Worshiping God with a heart overflowing with praise doesn't make you a follower of Christ. Telling people you're a Christian doesn't make you a follower of Christ. Studying your Bible doesn't make you a follower of Christ. Listening to Christian music and singing Christian songs and participating in Christian activities and putting a Christian bumper sticker on your car and hanging a cross around your neck and wearing a WWJD tee-shirt...none of it makes you a follower of Christ.

Only one thing makes you a disciple. Doing what Jesus said. *If you love Me, you will keep My commands.*

Read Matthew chapters 5-7, what we call the Sermon on the Mount. It's pretty practical stuff. And not really a lot of fun. Any thought that Jesus came to invite us to a celebration—a big happy worship service with lots of terrific music and a great life of fellowship, praising the Lord and getting "blessed" from morning till night—is immediately knocked out of our minds before we're 20 minutes into the New Testament. The "blessings" Jesus talks about in the beatitudes are quite different than that counterfeit thing commonly preached in our day that erroneously goes by the same name. We have twisted the Lord's words around to make them pleasing to our flesh. But listen to what He really said:

Rejoice when you're persecuted.

Don't call anyone foolish or make fun of them or you will be in danger of hell.

Don't so much as *think* an impure thought.

Let people strike you not once but twice without retaliating.

Not only give to those who ask from you, give *more* than they ask.

Love your enemies.

Pray for those who persecute you.

Be righteous in ways no one sees.

Don't worry about what's going to happen tomorrow.

Deal with your own sins before you think about the faults of others.

Anyone who thinks those kinds of things are either easy or fun hasn't tried them!

No party. Jesus calls us to follow His example into sonship.

Right here and now. Look up and around you...what do you see?...who are the men and women in your path? Your daughterhood or sonship can come alive nowhere else but right there, among those people and in those situations nearest at hand.

Twenty-one

To Whom Did Jesus Come?

WHEN JESUS CAME TO THE WORLD, HE DID NOT COME TO THE IMPERSON-
AL MASSES. He came to individuals...to me...to you.

There have always been crowds to follow Jesus, from the first century till now. History is full of them. Multitudes who watch full of curiosity
and amazement. There are a lot of good church people in the crowds too.

But the crowds remain largely oblivious to the deeper mission of
Jesus to this earth. They are just like those you perhaps saw in your imagination flocking out from your cities and towns and homes and work-
places. They are like the people bustling along beside me. They are
unaware of the high truth that He came to teach men and women to
become sons and daughters of His Father.

Jesus did not come to amass great multitudes.

He came to look *you and me* in the eye.

We are all part of the impersonal throng...until that fateful, defining
crossroads when He pauses, looks around, and His eyes lock into ours.

In that instant, the mission of Jesus to earth reaches its first climax.
For suddenly it has become a mission, not to the masses, not to the universe...but a mission to you.

"Come," He says. "I want you to follow Me."

When the swarm parts and those eyes of love and authority deliver
their divine invitation and command, from that moment the gospel
account becomes a very personal story.

You and I are no longer bystanders, curiosity-seekers, observers worrying about when or where we will eat lunch, or wondering what will become of our schedules and plans, our previous priorities and lifestyle.

None of those things matter now.

We have been *called.*

His eyes have sought ours, found them, penetrated into the depths of motive and will and life-priority...and He says, "Come."

No more will we follow at a distance. We have been invited into His circle...invited to listen, invited to share, invited to question. We have been beckoned into the inner sanctum of His presence.

You and I have been summoned to become the thirteenth disciple in that select company at the nucleus of the multitude.

Henceforth when He speaks...He is speaking to us...to *you and me.*

He has invited us to share intimacy with Him...so that He might tell us of His mission, and so that we might participate in it.

You men—and I include myself—He has called you, not to manhood...but to become sons.

You women, He has called you, not to womanhood...but to become daughters.

Sons and daughters of obedience.

Twenty-two

The Signposts
at Crossroad One

EVERYONE FIRST ENCOUNTERS JESUS MORE OR LESS AS A STRANGER.

It was no accident that earlier I wrote, "We don't exactly even know who He is."

There is more truth to that statement than you may realize. Because the name *Jesus* is so familiar to the ears of our culture and spiritual background and training, we forget that we each come to Him as a stranger at first too.

That moment of eye contact—which in truth is not really eye contact at all, but *heart* contact—when He turns and isolates us in the crowd and speaks to our heart and says, "Come...I want *you* to follow Me," happens before we really know who He is.

It is a crossroad moment of life.

Though Jesus phrases it as a command, He is really asking a question. "Are you willing to come along...to take a chance...to follow a man you don't know very much about?"

I call it a question because His *"Come,"* demands a response. We must answer. And there are only two options—yes or no.

It is a crossroad. We will take one road or the other. We're going to take the road whose signpost is carved with the word *Yes*...or the one whose arrow points in the opposite direction that says *No*.

There are no other roads, no detours.

We witness each of the two responses throughout the gospels. We see those who follow, who drop their papers and pens and fishing nets and whatever else might be occupying their time and attention, and go.

Wherever Jesus is, we observe people walking up to those two signposts and looking them over. We see people pause when He asks the question, look in both directions, and then make their choice.

We can't see very far down the roads in either direction. We are told to count the cost. Yet this first crossroad moment comes before we really possess much information about just what that cost is.

Yet as Jesus encounters the men and women within the pages of the New Testament, He quickly moves them toward this important crossroads. Early in the story we begin to see the drama of the two responses repeated over and over. He doesn't explain. He doesn't spend a lot of time trying to convince them of the benefits of following. He simply brings them to the crossroad and says, "Come."

"As Jesus was walking beside the Sea of Galilee, He saw two brothers, Simon called Peter and his brother Andrew... '*Come, follow Me,*' Jesus said... At once they left their nets and followed Him" (Mt. 4:18-20).

Yes.

"He said to another man, 'Follow Me.' But the man replied, 'Lord, first let me go and bury my father' " (Lk. 9:59).

No.

He called the scribes and Pharisees too, with the same two responses.

"Then a teacher of the law came to Him and said, 'Teacher, I will follow You wherever You go' " (Mt. 8:19).

Yes.

"Then the Pharisees went out and began to plot with the Herodians how they might kill Jesus (Mk. 3:6).

No.

Early in the Gospels this is the persistent message, "*Follow Me.*" It continues all the way to the end—two thieves being crucified on either side of Him. Two responses. One *yes,* the other *no.*

Jesus constantly probes the crowd, looking for those willing to respond and ready to answer, "*Yes,* I am willing...*yes,* I want to follow...*yes,* I will leave my past life and go with You."

What did *you* leave behind when you obeyed the summons?

Or perhaps you are one still standing at the crossroad waiting to see which answer you will make.

Twenty-three

A Cluster
at Life's Intersection

IN CONSIDERING THE QUESTION AT THE FIRST CROSSROAD, I find the woman at the well of John 4 fascinating.

Though Jesus did not speak the same words to her that He did to His disciples, He nevertheless took her straight to the crossroad and confronted her with how she intended to respond to His call upon her life.

"If you knew the gift of God and who it is that asks you for a drink, you would have asked Him and He would have given you living water...whoever drinks the water I give Him will never thirst. Indeed, the water I give Him will become in Him a spring of water welling up to eternal life" (Jn. 4:10,14).

There it is. He takes her straight to the two signposts and puts before her a choice of responses. She could easily have said, "You're crazy, buddy. I don't know who You are, but I don't have to listen to this stuff."

But instead she ran excitedly back to town, spread the word about Him, and single-handedly set off a huge revival, if you want to call it that, throughout the region. Usually you have to read between the lines of the Gospels to discover the full story behind what is apparent on the surface. I don't know any way to read between the lines here but that this woman became a believer and perhaps one of the Lord's key followers in the area.

"Many of the Samaritans from that town believed in Him because of the woman's testimony...So when the Samaritans came to Him, they urged Him to stay with them, and He stayed two days. And...many more became believers. They said to the woman, 'We no longer believe just because of what you said; now we have heard for ourselves, and we know that this man really is the Savior of the world' " (Jn. 4:39-42).

That is pretty clear indication, as I read it, that this thirsty woman whose name we do not even know answered *Yes* to the divine, *"Come,"* when it suddenly intruded upon her life that day beside the well at the village of Sychar in Samaria.

But when we see the rich young ruler facing his crossroads moment, we observe a much different answer. Jesus always probes straight to the heart of our personal point of reluctance, pride, disobedience, and selfishness. With the woman, it was, "Go bring your husband." Her adultery was the point of sin which Jesus knew she had to confront. For the rich young ruler it was wealth.

When Jesus takes us to the crossroad, He doesn't fool around with superficialities.

" '...go, sell your possessions and give to the poor...Then come, follow Me.' When the young man heard this, he went away sad, because he had great wealth" (Mt. 19:21-22).

He spoke to no one, set off no revival, did not ask Jesus to stay two days.

There are always two responses.

God gave Adam and Eve free will in the garden, and that same free will was still intact when Jesus came as the Savior of the world. Here is the command, here is your opportunity, here is eternal life...you are free to choose. You may accept it. You may obey. But you are always free to walk away.

That's why the crowds came and went in Jesus' day, and come and go in ours. The two signposts are always in front of us. Yet as much as He is on the minds of the men and women of our world today, most never look to the signposts, never hear His voice as it softly beckons, "Come...I want you to follow Me."

The crowd is always with us, bustling and noisy, hearing on one level but not perceiving, His name on their lips but their ears plugged from really hearing His voice. Many come and go, never looking Jesus straight in the eye, playing the religion game, tinkering with spiritual things as if participating in a social club, forever clustering near the fork in the road but never embarking down the YES road of discipleship.

Indeed, many churches are built right at this crossroad. It is popular and inexpensive spiritual real estate. It is a nice and comfortable place to live...comfortable because the challenge is never given to answer YES.

They who remain here all their spiritual lives are those of whom Jesus spoke in the all-important parable of the sower. Jesus emphasized so urgently that His disciples listen and understand this particular parable because it explains the responses of people we see all around us every day. The parable of the sower is lived out every Sunday of every week in every church throughout the land. In the chairs and pews and pulpits beside you and in front of you and behind you sit the four kinds of human soil that Jesus described.

Which are you? What is growing out of the soil of your character—hundredfold fruit of God's Kingdom, or weeds and thorns?

The crowds don't understand Jesus' mission of sonship. How can they? They have never answered the summons. They remain forever clustered at the crossroad.

But in truth, remaining at the crossroad is just another way of answering No.

Many of you reading will long ago have left your nets. Just as many of you have probably been part of the crowd for many years. But there will come a time when that crowd will part, and He will slowly turn. Suddenly you will be aware that it is you His eyes have found in the midst of the multitude.

No longer will He be satisfied for you to remain one of the throng. He now wants you as His disciple.

Which of the two responses will be yours when that crossroad moment of contact comes between you and the man called Jesus Christ?

Will you follow...or turn your back and walk away?

"Come," He says, "I want *you* to follow Me."

Twenty-four

An Upside-down World

For those, perhaps few in number, who do respond to that call, who obey that summons, FOLLOW ME, Jesus will begin to teach many things about life as His follower in God's Kingdom.

Immediately after the Yes road has been taken, the crowds thin. Jesus then gets down to business with those who are in earnest about accompanying Him.

The gospel tone shifts. Jesus calls His disciples, and us with them, away to quiet places far removed from the throngs. Quickly His teaching begins to deepen.

Now that we have followed, He says, we must learn a whole new way of life. Things function differently in God's economy, He says. Values and attitudes are upside-down from what we have been accustomed to. Relationships operate according to different parameters. All of life is lived differently.

Imagine an unseen world where none of the old rules apply, where gravity makes things fall upward, where two plus two does not equal four, where there is no such thing as death, where slaves are honored and the rich and powerful are pitied, where to own nothing is considered success.

Think of your own examples. The important point is that the divine mathematics and economics of this new place are upside-down from everything in this world we live in.

That's a little like what Jesus is talking about in the Sermon on the Mount. "When you become My disciple," he says, "*everything* changes."

The equations of life become fundamentally altered, the equal signs are drawn differently.

You must become a different kind of person altogether—think differently, respond differently, relate to people differently, approach life differently on every level. It will not happen all at once. It is a growth process. But that is the program you've set yourself when you answer Yes and come on the road of discipleship with Him.

That's why you must be born again into this new world. It is so different that the transformation must be total. There is no other way to live in this new Kingdom except by a complete transformation of your outlook.

A great many in our day erroneously confuse this being born again Jesus speaks of with a one-time experience—a commitment made at a church or evangelistic service, baptism, an intellectual decision regarding the truth of Jesus' claims in the New Testament, or a prayer of repentance and acceptance. Whether or not such criteria are to be found in the Gospels is not the point of this discussion. What is the point is that this is not what Jesus speaks to Nicodemus about, but rather the transition into this new world where His Father's principles rule.

To become a citizen of that world means laying down all claim to the former ways. There is no such thing as being "born again" through the experience of a moment while the mathematics and economics of the former world still reign—where the equal signs in life remain the same, where relationships still function as before, where motives are unchanged, where decisions are made as always, where your rights still dominate your thinking, and where the independence of self-rule remains the guiding principle.

That's the same as saying, "I've been born again but haven't been born again. I've accepted the new world but am keeping my citizenship in the old."

Praying a prayer or going forward at a meeting or being baptized cannot make you a citizen of that upside-down Kingdom of Jesus' Father. Only the relinquishment of the right to self-rule, and taking the will of the Father instead, can do that.

Such a relinquishment can begin in a moment. And thus momentary experiences are often important to signal a commitment to such change. But only if they lead to a permanent *transfer of citizenship* out of one kingdom and into another.

That's why there soon comes a second crossroad that is imperative to your spiritual future. That's where we have to face the all-important issue of *rule*—who is going to be master of my life.

Now it becomes a question of lordship.

Twenty-five

The Question
at Crossroad Two

Ultimately the most important issue all must face in this new Kingdom is a question of identity.

"Who is this man Jesus whom we have followed?"

So when Jesus turns to us a second time, finds our eyes and probes even more deeply than before, it is to ask the very personal question upon which the rest of our life will hinge, "*Who do you say that I am?*"

"Not who does everyone else think I am...but who am I in *your* life?"

It comes to each of us. It is the second important crossroad in our spiritual pilgrimage with Jesus Christ.

Again there are two responses. We witness the stark contrast between them most visibly in the two disciples, men who must have been friends, who must have discussed these things together, both leaders among the Twelve—*Peter* the acknowledged spokesman, and *Judas* the keeper of the purse.

Think about it...Judas was with Jesus and the other eleven for three years. They were friends. They laughed and talked and grew together. Judas went out with the rest when Jesus commissioned them as apostles. He told people about Jesus, probably healed and worked miracles according to the Gospel writers. Judas was no "bad apple" among them. He was no outcast, no black sheep of the group right from the beginning. Think of it—Judas cast out demons and healed the sick and preached that people should believe in Jesus! None of the disciples knew what was coming. He was one of them.

Yet eventually came the moment of truth...for Peter...for Judas.

When that crossroad came, though he fumbled along with many stumbles and blunders along the way, Peter recognized who Jesus was, and knew what that realization meant in his life.

Judas, however, though he answered Yes to the initial summons, never figured out what *Son of God* and *Lord* meant. He did not allow the teaching to do its deeper work. And so when the second crossroad came, he could not reply.

He didn't know who Jesus was.

Following is a necessary starting point on the road to discipleship. But it isn't enough. Eventually comes the question of rule and lordship.

Who is in charge? Who calls the shots? Who makes the decisions?

There can be only one master in any life. Therefore, ultimately all who take the first road arrive at length at a second crossroad..."*Who do you say that I am?*"

For Peter, it came on the road to Caesarea Philippi. I think for Judas that moment came as Jesus looked him in the eye at the last supper when He dipped the bread in the dish and gave it to him.

"Judas," He said, pleading one last time with His eyes, "it is still not too late to be born into the Kingdom of My Father. You've followed, you've been My disciple. But you've never truly relinquished self-rule to My lordship in your life. You still have not given up your goals, your plans, your desire to make things happen your own way. It's not too late, Judas...who do you say that I am?"

But Judas could not give the one and only thing that ultimately mattered—himself. He could not give up the right to sit on the throne of his life as his own master.

Self-rule is really the only thing any of us have to give that is truly our own. It is the one commodity, controlled by the free will God gave us, over which we have total control. Thus, the yielding of it is the greatest gift we have to offer.

And in the relinquishment of self-rule do we cease to be independent entities, and make ourselves sons and daughters.

Peter gave it. In his unbounded enthusiasm, he was always stumbling over his tongue. But his heart was full of the desire to give Jesus complete and total lordship.

"Lord, don't wash only my feet, but my hands and head as well!" (see Jn. 13:9)

With all the energy of his being, Peter hungered to be God's man in every part of his life. He wanted sonship!

But not Judas.

Faced with the same decision, Judas chose to keep himself sitting on that seat of rule. He had followed at the first crossroad, but he had not truly made Jesus his Lord in the new Kingdom. He had not relinquished self-rule.

It is possible to be a follower, even a disciple on one level, but never to have made that transition into the new operating mechanics of God's Kingdom.

Churches are built here too, further along toward discipleship, perhaps, but reluctant to look beyond their ceaseless activities of supposed ministry to confront the full reality of what Jesus' Sonship means—self-denial. It is fearfully easy to give Jesus our worship and praise, without following Him past this important crossroad into obedient Sonship.

Being born again isn't a matter of salvation as much as it is a question of: Have you made the transition out of the old into the new?

The crossroad moment came for Judas that night at the table. Then he got up, and went out. And the Gospel writer John captures the dark poignancy of his fateful choice:

"As soon as Judas had taken the bread, he went out. *And it was night*" (Jn. 13:30, emphasis added).

What will be our choice when we face that question, "Who do you say that I am? Am I your *Lord*...or will you go out into the night...into the darkness...alone?"

The difference between Peter and Judas is the difference between sonship and betrayal, between *yes* and *no* at Crossroad Two.

We must figure out who Jesus Christ is in our lives—an acquaintance, a friend, someone we follow because He is a dynamic leader and fun to be around...or Son of God and Lord.

Twenty-six

The Ultimate—
Crossroad Three

Again a winnowing comes.

A third crossroad arrives for those who choose to call Jesus *Lord*. This time the question is more piercing yet, probing to the utter depths of the heart and soul.

Not many churches border the discipleship road in this region to which we have now come. Those few that stake their claim here are made up of men and women who understand the true cost of bringing the gospel into every corner of life.

At the first crossroad throngs and crowds gather about it. Crossroad question one is put before the whole world. Will they have ears to hear it?

At the second crossroad, we are one among a select company of disciples. Crossroad question two confronts those who have become Christ's followers—will they make Him lord?

But thereafter the crowds thin and finally when the third crossroad comes...we stand alone. It is just *you* and Jesus...and *me* and Jesus. He looks into your eyes. His question is meant for your ears alone.

At last have we arrived at life's ultimate crossroad.

How much are we willing to lay down? To what extent will we relinquish what we call *ourselves*? How far are we willing to take discipleship?

What are the limits of the lordship we turn over to Him? How much will we hold back? How much of our selves will we try to preserve and keep alive?

113

Crossroad question three is stark and unyielding:

"Are you willing to die with Me?"

After Judas went out, Peter spoke bravely and enthusiastically. "I am ready to go with You to prison. I will go with You all the way! Even if all the others fall away, I will not. I will never leave You!"

Ah, Peter, Jesus must have thought, *courageous words. But you know not what you speak. The final test is the **ultimate** test. Are you truly willing to go **that** far?*

Are we not all like dear Peter, full of enthusiastic words of commitment whose implications we scarcely fathom?

For even Peter, who had come through the first two crossroads with flying colors despite his stumbles and foibles, wasn't quite ready for what would confront him later that night and the next day. Even Peter wasn't yet strong enough in his faith to answer Yes to the final demand upon his discipleship at Crossroad Three.

If we're honest, you and I probably have to admit that we are no more ready than he. When that moment of truth comes, do we not, each in our own way, deny Him too rather than go all the way to Golgotha with Him?

As Jesus carries His cross through the streets, where are His disciples to help Him bear it?

Nowhere to be found. It is Simon of Cyrene whose shoulders and back must be commandeered into divine service. But the disciples have all fled. Peter turned and ran. "I don't know Him!" he shouts as he disappears in the crowd.

Have we not all done the same, maybe not with shouts but with whispered denials no one ever hears?

But Peter grew ready in time, as must all who would follow His example.

"Peter," says the Lord, "are you willing to die with me?"

"Michael Phillips," He says, "are *you* willing...?"

"Reader of Michael Phillips's words, are *you* willing...?"

How personal do we want to get? If the Samaritan woman had her personal point of hesitation, her own inner *No* that Jesus addressed...and if the rich young ruler had his individual *No* which his unique crossroad confronted…what about you and me?

What is the death to which He calls *us,* dear friend? Speaking for myself, I think perhaps I could more easily answer *Yes* to the question, "Are you willing to die with Me?" than to, "Are you willing for one of your children to turn his back on a relationship with you because of Me?"

I cannot answer Yes to that question. As aware as I am of Jesus' statement, "He who loves…more than Me…" I still cannot say *Yes* to the Lord at that point.

I confess, I am *not* yet fully willing. Such is the painful and daily reality of *my* Crossroad Three. What is yours?

There is a clear and visible progression in the Gospel account, through which Jesus takes those who would be His disciples.

You and I are among that number now. We can no longer sit around on the fringes and pretend His words are meant for everyone else. They are directed straight at us.

Once we come to grips with who He is, immediately Jesus explains what that means.

And what it means is death, nothing more, nothing less.

Is it a literal death to which He calls us?

Not usually. In some eras such has indeed been required of His servants. But for most who would be His followers, it is death to self, to motives of self, to attitudes of self, to reputation, and to the rule of self, exactly as Jesus said. And sometimes it means death to dreams.

The death is to independence…to rights…to rule. How much are you willing to give up?

"I tell you the truth, anyone who will not receive the Kingdom of God like a little child will never enter it" (Mk. 10:15).

If we want to be part of the crowd, a Christian groupie, a hanger-on, then we can pretend that the Kingdom of God is a celebration, party, a worship concert.

If we want to be followers of Jesus as He taught His disciples, then we are joining a funeral march. It leads out of Jerusalem to a lonely hill called Calvary. And we cannot always pick and choose the kind of nails that will be used when our turn comes to follow His example.

115

This message is so foundational to what Jesus had to teach that the first three Gospel writers repeat it almost word for word. It is *the* central impact of the gospel story.

> *From that time on Jesus began to explain to His disciples that He must go to Jerusalem and suffer many things at the hands of the elders, chief priests and teachers of the law, and that He must be killed and on the third day be raised to life...*
>
> *Then Jesus said to His disciples,* **"If anyone would come after Me, he must deny himself and take up his cross and follow Me. For whoever wants to save his life will lose it, but whoever loses his life for Me will find it"** *(Matthew 16:21,24-25, emphasis added).*

> *He then began to teach them that the Son of Man must suffer many things and be rejected by the elders, chief priests and teachers of the law, and that He must be killed and after three days rise again.*
>
> **"If anyone would come after Me, he must deny himself and take up his cross and follow Me. For whoever wants to save his life will lose it, but whoever loses his life for Me and for the gospel will save it"** *(Mark 8:31,34b-35, emphasis added).*

> *And he said, "The Son of Man must suffer many things and be rejected by the elders, chief priests and teachers of the law, and he must be killed and on the third day be raised to life." Then He said to them all:* **"If anyone would come after Me, he must deny himself and take up his cross daily and follow Me. For whoever wants to save his life will lose it, but whoever loses his life for Me will save it"** *(Luke 9:22-24, emphasis added).*

Therefore, ultimately the decisive question comes to all His followers: *Are you willing to lay everything in this life down...put to death all claim to what this life has to offer...abandon all thought of being in charge of your own affairs again...crucify every attitude and priority and motive of your own and take the sermon on the mount as your job description for the rest of life?*

The singular importance of this crossroads moment clarifies why Jesus had to rebuke Peter after his triumphant confession of Him as the

Christ. Because the necessary next step after that realization, as clearly and necessarily as night follows day, is self-denial and death. Peter tried to block that all-important progression. He recognized who Jesus was, but remained unseeing of what it meant. He was still suffering from the erroneous conclusions of centuries of rabbinical teaching about the Messiah from the Old Testament, that the Christ would come as a conquering earthly king.

"No," says Jesus, "you are looking at it through man's eyes not God's. Remember, things are different in God's Kingdom. Everything works differently. My Father will conquer sin by invading the enemy's house differently than the world would, not with legions of earthly might, but by sonship, by obedient abandonment of the will of a Son into the will of a Father.

"By yielding to death will death be defeated. What you are looking at, Peter, is the world's way, satan's way. But it is not God's way. Listen! This is how salvation comes in my Father's economy.

"And He began to teach them..."

It is the necessary progression. *"The Son of God must suffer...be rejected...and die. If anyone would come after Me, he must deny himself...and follow Me."*

Sonship means nothing less than relinquishment—even of life itself. If you would be sons and daughters, this is the formula.

These three crossroad questions mark out the inevitable progression of our footsteps if we would follow Jesus all the way to the cross.

PART 3

An Obedient Son

Twenty-seven

Angel or Man?

From what we know, angels are celestial beings different from humans in many respects. Angels are clearly not mortal. Some theologians point to another important distinction as well—that angels do not possess free will.

These things are difficult to understand because they are not made clear in the Scriptures. We also know that there are fallen angels. How did these angels fall unless they had free will? Therefore, it is clear that all the intricacies of exactly what comprises the nature of the angelic personality we do not and cannot know with certainty.

If the word *angel* literally means a "messenger," a significant question is this: Why did God not send an angel to do the work instead of the Son? God sent angels to earth many times before with important communications for the men and women of earth. Why did not an angel come to deliver the good news regarding the Kingdom of God and to tell mankind about life in it?

Would that not perhaps have been much simpler and more straightforward? Would people not have been more inclined to listen? Even the Pharisees could hardly have argued had Gabriel or Michael stood at the door of the Temple with a message directly from God.

Why, then, did God disguise the messenger so thoroughly that no one knew who He was?

Would not an angel have been the perfect being to announce the news? *The Kingdom of God is at hand. Repent and believe.*

Why wasn't Jesus an angel?

The answer, I think, is to be found precisely in those two differences between angels and men. As men and women ourselves, we had to see how a mortal man, with free will just like ours, could *choose* to lay down and relinquish that will.

No angel could face that moral dilemma, that free intellectual and emotional choice.

Only a mortal man could *choose* childship in the midst of the temptations that make fallen humanity what it is, full of internal urges to exalt self and to exercise the self-rule of independent manhood. In the midst of those human pressures, only a mortal man with free will could *choose* sonship.

No angel could make such a choice.

If the example was one that would get all the way inside us and truly transform us, we had to do more than just *hear* the message announced. We had to see it exampled. We had to know that it could be done, that the mortal will of self really and truly could be laid down and submitted to One higher.

An angel could *tell* us to do it. But only a man could *show* us how.

So God became a man.

What a stupendous thing!

Jesus was *born* as the Son of God, but He *grew up* as a man.

Not a pretend man or an 80 percent man...but a *real* man. With *real* struggles. With a *real* will that wanted its own way just as do all human wills.

Can you grasp the enormity of this? We tend to lay a gloss over the humanity of Jesus, thinking that it was somehow *easier* for Him to lay down His will. We turn Him into a sort of half-man, half-angel in our minds.

Angels have no will to lay down. But Jesus did. And it was 100 percent a mortal, human will.

So as Jesus grew and matured from an infant into a boy, then into a youth, then into a young man, and finally into a mature man...His human will was fully alive, fully developed as a *human* will.

122

Jesus *wanted* His own way. We know that from His prayer in Gethsemane. He had to struggle just as we do to lay that will down.

Because of His goodness, I'm sure He was mocked and made fun of as a boy. Was that *easy* for Him? Not by any means. I'm sure it was a great struggle for His youthful flesh.

He became an adult just as we do. His earthly father died. He took over the carpentry responsibilities. As the eldest, He became head of the family. Think of it—Jesus actually may have run a family business. He had customers. He had to handle financial decisions. He had to provide for His mother. Can you imagine Jesus sending a statement of how much was due on someone's account? What did Jesus do when a customer didn't pay for work as agreed upon? It was no halo existence. He lived a real life.

Finally He became an adult *man*. Not an angel.

And then, after growing into adulthood, He had to humble Himself, subserving His own will to the Father's, and become a child yet again, laying down the mortal manhood with which He had been invested through the miracle of the incarnation, and die into the will of God the Father.

It was no cheap death to self, no easy relinquishment, no automatic abandonment of the will of His manhood. It was all that death to self-rule is for any man or woman.

Twenty-eight

What Really Happened at Bethlehem?

THEOLOGIANS HAVE DEVISED ALL SORTS OF CONTORTED WAYS to explain the incarnation that make little sense to anyone but themselves. But I see only two possible ways to account for the astounding fact that God became a man in the person of Jesus Christ.

One, that when He left Heaven for earth, the Son took along a little something to help Him out during the tough times, to insure that this grand experiment was a success. He brought a little piece of His divinity along with Him to prevent His being *fully* subjected to the sinful plight of man. That, after all, might have been too great a risk.

Lucifer had rebelled. Adam had failed. Eve had disobeyed. Beings with free will, they each exalted themselves above obedience to their Creator. Following them, the ten commandments had failed. The Israelites had failed. Even faithful old Moses failed. So now, when it came time for the Son to go to earth, it would be best to *insure* the salvation of mankind, taking no chances that something might go wrong again.

So maybe a little something "extra" was smuggled into the stable that night at Bethlehem.

I mean no sacrilege whatsoever, but there are many well-meaning Christians who envision the infant Jesus being born with halo on his head and a tiny magic wand in His hand, which through His life was the link to His divinity, giving Him supernatural insight, supernatural power, and supernatural victory over sin. It was the divine insurance policy to make sure *this* plan for the salvation of the world came off without a hitch.

No one would admit to such a belief. But practically, this is really how they see it, that Jesus was born a human, but not *quite* a human, not *really* like us. It is the representation of Jesus from the old medieval paintings with a sheen around His head, the Christ image that glows in the dark, complete with halo, floating six inches off the ground.

It's also the Jesus of 21st-century evangelicalism. Protestantism, Anglicanism, Catholicism, and Orthodoxy, if you follow some of our theologies all the way to the end. Jesus who "saves" mankind with a kind of divine magic wand. Say the right incantations, go through the right rituals, pray according to the right doctrinal patterns—every Christian sect and denomination from evangelicalism to Catholicism has its own spiritual formulas—and *poof!* salvation is granted.

Honestly, I say these things not lightly at all, but with tears welling up in my eyes at how much Christendom has trivialized the great work of Christ into *formulae*, and into a sort of celestial magic. As much as we recoil from that word, I use it intentionally, if for no other reason than to shock us awake to the reality of illogical doctrines. Our explanations demean both Jesus and the cross, and prevent the reality of His life and work from penetrating into the world. We've got to be honest with ourselves and recognize that this is what some of our pronouncements sound like to the world. And it's why the world is not really listening to the gospel in a widespread way. In actual practice, we have turned the salvation of God into a spiritual magic act, each branch of Christianity with its own recipe. No wonder the world is confused by the many different salvation languages we speak.

The second way to interpret the incarnation is much different. It is this: That Jesus was born *fully* a man. No magic wand, no halo. He didn't glow in the dark. He didn't float six inches off the ground. His muscles got tired. His feet sweat. His body had the same organs and glands that ours do. He went to the bathroom. He got hungry and thirsty. His hair got dirty. He possessed intellect and emotions. He had the capacity to get exasperated at His disciples, angry at the Pharisees, and afraid for what He might have to face as the cross neared. Most importantly, He was born with a fully developed free will of humanity.

I see no other choices. Either Jesus was a *man*. Or He was an almost-man, a God-man who had brought along a get-out-of-jail-free card with Him.

Now in truth He *was* a God-man, the Divine Man. But not in the way many people view the two components of His nature interrelating. We mustn't let His divinity obscure the totality of His manhood. We can't let our imaginations smuggle a magic wand in among the swaddling clothes in the manger at Bethlehem.

Nor can we put a little baby angel into Mary's arms as we picture the thing in our minds, a being *incapable* of sin because of His heavenly origins. To do either will irreparably constrict our capacity to grasp the enormity of Christ's Saviorhood. Mary held no infant angel that night in Bethlehem, but a tiny *boy*...her own son, and God's own Son.

"For the divine nature was His from the first; yet He...emptied Himself, taking the very nature of a slave. Bearing the human likeness, revealed in human shape, He humbled Himself and became obedient..." (see Phil. 2:6-7, NIV, NAS, NEB).

He *emptied* Himself of His divinity, humbled Himself, and took the form of man.

Jesus came to us *fully* as a human being.

Twenty-nine

A Progressively
Revealed Sonship

JESUS WAS A MAN, NOT AN ANGEL. HE POSSESSED A WILL that was His own. He possessed the capacity of choice that was human. And He won His Sonship, and our salvation, by exercising that choice.

I repeat yet again because it is so foundational—Jesus was fully a man. He did not have to be perfect. He *chose* to be perfect every day of His life. He chose, by the continuous exercise of His free will, to subserve that will to the Father's, every moment of every day of His life.

What a truly extraordinary thing, that Jesus did not *have* to be perfect. He chose to lay down His will, to relinquish all but the Father's will, and He did so for us, so that we might be able to follow Him straight into the heart of the Father.

So we truly do walk in His footsteps through these three difficult but necessary progressions of faith we have looked at:

Come...Who am I?...Are you willing to die?

As we encounter them in our lives, therefore, Jesus is truly with us, going before us, because He has actually faced these questions Himself.

Does it shock some of you when I say that Jesus had to face this progression of dawning revelation in His life too?

Can you grasp the import of the fact that Jesus had to answer the crossroads questions of steadily deepening commitment to God's purpose just like we do? He had to wrestle with what it meant to *follow* His Father

129

all the way. He had to come to grips with the most essential question of His life, *who* He was. And He ultimately had to pray, to the point of sweating blood, to be willing to *die*.

No magic wand, no halo, no get-out-of-jail-free card...but real humanity.

As I said at the beginning, we suffer from so many images and pre-conceptions about Jesus that we aren't even aware when they block a deep understanding of His true character. The fact is, there was a time when Jesus *didn't* know that He was the Son of God. At two or three years of age, if He was fully a human being and subject to the limitations of humanity, He could not possibly have known.

When did He begin to realize that something unusual was happening within Him? Did Mary tell Him of the angel's visit? How old might He have been at the time?

What did Jesus know and when did He know it, is one of the most fascinating theological questions of all time. How did He grow into the awareness that He was unlike anyone who had ever lived? Did that awareness begin to dawn at five...perhaps ten?

Certainly by the age of twelve it was well developed, but still not complete. By then He knew that God was truly His Father, an enormous revelation that most of Israel's rabbis hadn't yet figured out. Yet still the boy Jesus had much farther to go before He would grasp the fullness of what His Christness meant. Even at twelve, after all, He was still a boy, and not yet ready to be Savior of the world.

When did that greater revelation come...at eighteen...at twenty-five? And *how* did it come? Suddenly or by slow degrees?

Such an inquiry may at first seem a trivial curiosity. Yet I think that when one probes more deeply into it, these questions tug at the foundations of the incarnation itself. How one approaches this question of *knowing*, the awareness of His Christness, plumbs the very depths of the intricate relationship between Father and Son. Who really *was* it who walked in the garden in the cool of the day? Who was it who said, "Let *Us* create man in *Our* image"? And back further still, *Who* was it who created the heavens and the earth: the Father, the Father and Son and Spirit somehow working in tandem, or simply...*God*?

But though we cannot fully know such unknowables, we can take enormous comfort and strength from the realization that the same progression of dawning revelation that we go through came in Jesus's life too. He faced a series of crossroads just as we do. We cannot apprehend exactly what they were or when they occurred. But Jesus steadily stepped into His Sonship as it slowly was revealed by God's Spirit within Him. He had to exercise the free will of His humanity to *choose* to live that Sonship to the extent of the revelation as it came.

The temptation in the wilderness represented a great crossroad as Jesus prepared for his Messiah-ship. Then the baptism...and the voice of God saying, "This is My beloved Son in whom I am well pleased. Listen to Him."

The culmination had at last come in this lifelong process during which, in a sense, Jesus progressively *became* our Savior. He was always God's Son, of course. But He didn't enter into the fullness of that Sonship all at once after emptying Himself of His divinity. He had to *become* a Son by the exercise of His free will, capable of laying down His life for the sins of the world.

Therefore, wherever and whenever we face our crossroads, He can help us through them because He has been there Himself.

As with the rich young ruler, however, when that crucial moment comes, He must simply look into our eyes, put to us the probing question, then wait. At that moment, we are alone with our choice.

Our wills are free to go either direction too.

Thirty

The Divine Risk

Here is the crux of attempting to grasp the enormity of what Jesus did. All real wills can go in either direction. They don't *have* to make the right choice. There is no coercion. That is the definition of *free* will. It is truly free to choose.

If Jesus hadn't had free will, He would have been an angel. But by virtue of His manhood, He *did* possess free will. He didn't simply grow up and switch on the divine part of His nature. He had to *choose* sonship

The implication of this choosing is enormous. It means that when Jesus came to earth, His decisions could have gone either way. Salvation wasn't a done deal until the final moment when He breathed His last and gave up His mortality, ready to return again to the place of His origin at the Father's side. In other words, for 33 years, in a sense, the fate of the world's salvation hung in the balance.

Think what an astounding thing it would have been had Jesus failed.

Does the question almost ring with blasphemy in your ears? Was such impossible?

I do not think so. Otherwise He would have been an angel. But He was a man with a fully operational and human free will. By definition this means that all the way to the end, His will was alive. He *could* have ended His garden prayer with, "Forget it...I can't do this anymore."

God does not play games.

When we are told that Jesus was "tempted," that means He was tempted. Really and truly tempted. His mortal human will was taken to the limit and *tempted*! It was no fake or shallow temptation, but the real thing.

What an incredible thing that God placed free will in the very center of creation. In free will we see God's great risk, and his willingness to take such a risk. A huge risk...the ultimate risk. The first Adam was also God's son, a perfect being. But somehow God thought the risk worth it to give Adam self-will, knowing that it *could* be fatal.

And as it turned out...it was fatal. The first Adam gave in to the temptation. He chose self will and independence rather than obedience. His fall introduced sin into the world of man.

With the failure of Eden so catastrophic, therefore, one might think God would send an angel, even a troop of angels, to redeem the world from this sin, just to make sure nothing could go wrong again. A man had failed once. It might be best to take no chances this second time with the weak, mortal, human vessel that had proved itself so unreliable through-out history.

But God chose to enter the human form Himself, and work the salvation and reconciliation of the universe through the mortal instrument of that phenomenal thing He had given only to the human creature in all the universe—*free will.*

He would accomplish salvation through Sonship...obedient Sonship. A Sonship won by the self-willed abandonment of independent rule.

All creation hung in the balance when satan came to Jesus. Because Jesus could have succumbed to the temptation.

They were real temptations. What if He had given in as had the first Adam?

Jesus went out into the desert a man, a human, a mortal...and He came back a true Son. Self-will relinquished...His manhood subserved to the Father...a child again. The curse of the first Adam had begun to be broken by the obedience of the second Adam.

But it was no automatic Sonship.

It was a Sonship of obedient choice, hard won by a free will wearing the mortal clothes of humanity. Jesus brought out no tricks to lessen the battle over self-rule, to make the temptations easier, to make Him a little *more* God and a little *less* man.

He had to win through that battle *as a man*.

And He went all the way to the cross having to fight that internal battle, knowing that He *could* give in at any time. He Himself said that He didn't *have* to die, that He could call down 12 legions of angels to deliver Him.

But He fought that battle *for us*, so that we too could become sons and daughters, so that we too could pray the prayer, "Not my will but Yours be done."

An angel could have told us to pray that prayer. But when we see Jesus pray it, in all the human agony of knowing a terrible death awaited Him, what can we do but fall on our knees and pray it with Him?

And when Jesus cried, "It is finished," what a triumphant cry it was. He had lived out His obedient human Sonship to the end.

The curse of sin was broken indeed!

Thirty-one

Magician or Son?

THE IDEA OF A PROGRESSIVELY DAWNING REVELATION OF SONSHIP IN THE
LIFE OF JESUS, and the notion that He *could* have made different choices
than He did, will undoubtedly cause some to squirm.

It will be hard for many to lay aside their halo images.

There are believers—though they would never recognize it—who do
not see Jesus as a real human mortal but someone they *call* a "man" but
who really wasn't like us at all.

That Jesus *could* have failed will be a scandalous notion in their ears.
That He actually had to choose to lay down a mortal will that wanted its
own way will seem incredible.

It is clearly outside the scope of this book to attempt a thorough discussion of what actually was "accomplished" on the cross by the death
and resurrection of Jesus in dealing the death blow to sin and bringing salvation and eternal life to mankind. I will not try to pinpoint with theological precision exactly *why* and *how* eternal life with God is ours. These
are great mysteries in the heavenly realms which, for reasons of His own,
God has kept obscure to our finite human hearts and intellects.

They remain mysteries to me as well, which is the reason I am reluctant to make too many absolute statements beyond my conviction that
God's goodness must be far greater than we can imagine. If more of those
who had set themselves to explain God's ways through the years had
devoted a greater portion of their energies to obey what He has told them
to do rather than theorize concerning His work, the world would doubtless
be much further along toward its ultimate salvation than it presently is.

If my words in this book are to have any lasting impact in your life, and if the writing of it is to have impact in my own, it will be because we are both turned more diligently to *do* what Jesus said, not because together we devise explanations pleasing to our intellects about His life and work, and the miracle of His death and resurrection.

I would only hope to challenge you, as I challenge myself, to take that death into your consciousness every moment of every day, so that the life! of the resurrection—a resurrection into childship—might be the reality in which you live and breathe and have your being.

To do this, it may help us to look at Christ's death briefly. Not to devise a theology about it...but in order to invite its unexplainable miracle more deeply into our hearts, and thus allow it the more thoroughly to empower us to live as God's sons and daughters.

Let us affirm at the outset that the life-changing miracle wrought at Calvary was accomplished by a *Son* not a magician. Sin was defeated by obedient Sonship, not divine magic. And though the mere suggestion of such a comparison will be regarded as shocking, much of the prevailing fundamental theology of the atonement reduces the cross to an illogical fiat accomplished as divine pixie dust is sprinkled on the "undeserving" because Christ "sacrificed Himself for them." It is a dissonant theologic equation, as explained by our modern-day doctors of the law, that *reduces* the atonement rather than elevates it to a wonderful and glorious expression of God's love. Such theologies appear scriptural because they follow its letter. They do not, however, conform to its deeper intent. Neither are they compassionate or in harmony with the character of God as revealed continuously from the first page of Genesis to the last page of Revelation.

Jesus Christ sacrificed Himself, to be sure. But it must mean more than many of our theologian-scribes would have it.

Can you dare venture boldly with me up the hill to Calvary, again as an invisible 13th disciple, to see if we might there discover, not some magic blood that covers us in spite of our sin, but the real blood of a real Sonship in which we may fully participate? Let us thus, with the Spirit of God inside us, and with the Sonship power of Jesus going before us, deal the death blow to sin in the relinquished sacrifice that gives life to our own sonship and daughterhood. Can you summon the courage to climb the sacred hill with me?

There are generally two broad views concerning Christ's death.

Even this simplification will be rejected by many who do not find their pet explanation adequately represented. I would nevertheless identify what I call primarily a *spiritual* interpretation and what I call a *secular* interpretation.

In the first, *God* is the prime mover. Man can do nothing to save himself. Man is doomed in his sin and deserving of punishment and death. But God has stepped in, and, though man does not deserve it, has provided a remedy, a ram in the bushes, by which we can be saved. That remedy is the cross of Christ.

In the more secular view, *man* is the prime mover in his salvation. True, we are not all as good as we ought to be. But if we try to follow the example of Jesus, and live a pretty good life, everything will be sorted out fairly by God in the end.

Taking the spiritual view, having cut ourselves off from God, all mankind deserves to be punished for its sin and ultimately to die. But because of His perfection, Jesus has taken that punishment upon Himself. By Christ's substitutionary death in our stead, those who "believe" and "accept" Him and "trust" in Him for their salvation will be granted eternal life rather than the death and punishment their sins deserve. According to this spiritual perspective, what kind of a life one lives has less to do with the mechanics of salvation than whether one believes in and accepts Jesus' salvation personally. Belief and spiritual formula are more pivotal than lifestyle, as evidenced by the creed, "You cannot live a good enough life to get into Heaven."

Those holding such a view say that if the belief-formula is adhered to, and a salvation prayer is prayed, if the correct rituals are followed— granting that there are a hundred or more different such rituals Christians hold, from very "spiritual" evangelical rituals to Catholic and very "church" based rituals—then salvation is granted immediately.

It is explained as a "spiritual transaction," a bargain, so to speak, in which God allows the death of Jesus to "pay the price" for our sins. God's holiness, which cannot abide in the presence of sin, is thus not compromised. He takes the life of His Son instead as the necessary payment, the required sacrifice, for the sin of the world. In order to avail ourselves of this salvation, we must enter into the transaction with God, first by repenting of our sin, then "accepting, trusting, believing, and receiving" Jesus Christ as Savior. This repentance and acceptance atonement enables Christ's blood spiritually to cleanse us from our sin, and allows us to enter into eternal life.

The other and more liberal view looks not so much to the "substitutionary" work but rather to the "example" of Jesus's death. A personal salvation experience and repentance prayer is less important than that we live out that *example* in our own daily lives—obeying His teaching, denying ourselves, putting others first, etc. A "spiritual experience" is less significant than that we do our best to live as Jesus taught. Lifestyle and choices rather than particular formula of salvation, is everything.

People have been arguing for centuries along the broad continuum between these two poles about what constitutes salvation. Is belief enough? Is repentance enough? Is a good life or motive enough? Is the cross the vehicle for a necessary "vicarious sacrifice" to appease the wrath of a holy God against sin...or is it a "symbol," an example of self-denial to be followed?

C.S. Lewis, with his great intellect and logical mind, cleverly avoided the criticism that comes to anyone who tries to be specific in this regard, by not trying to describe the *how* at all, and simply saying, "It works."

"The central Christian belief," wrote Lewis in his classic *Mere Christianity*, "is that Christ's death has somehow put us right with God and given us a fresh start. Theories as to how it did this are another matter. A good many theories have been held as to how it works; what all Christians are agreed on is that it does work...We are told that Christ was killed for us, that His death has washed out our sins, and that by dying He disabled death itself. That is the formula. That is Christianity...Any theories we build up as to how Christ's death did all this are...not to be confused with the thing itself."[1]

1. *Mere Christianity*, C.S. Lewis, 1943, 1945, 1952 by The MacMillian Publishing Co., New York, pp. 47-8.

Who can argue with such logic? He is probably nearer the truth than 98 percent of the treatises ever written and sermons ever preached on the atonement.

I suspect the actual truth of the work of the cross lies somewhere between the extremes of "formula-belief" and "exampled lifestyle." Both an overly "spiritualized" and an overly "secularized" view of the atonement in and of themselves are incomplete and will lead to the two common opposite errors of James 2:17-18.

We have to take the Lord's death inside. We have to die *with* Him. Neither baptism, a prayer of salvation, going forward at an evangelistic service, or 30 years faithful attendance at mass or the 11 o'clock worship service will accomplish that. Nor will living a good, moral life.

The blood of Jesus isn't some kind of red pixie dust sprinkled down from Heaven during a prayer of a salvation or at the moment of baptism or confirmation or when someone walks forward at a Billy Graham crusade to "confess Christ as Savior."

At such a moment, childship has only begun. The first crossroads question—

Will you follow?

—has been answered.

Yes, I will come.

But it is only the *first* crossroad. We then have to begin a lifelong process of appropriating Christ's Sonship for ourselves. We have to die to self-rule. This is where salvation comes alive, in the new birth into the Kingdom of the Father's—a new Kingdom where self no longer rules.

Something happened when Jesus was in the grave, something miraculous, something divine. Yes, a divine transaction occurred that no "good life" can apprehend or replace.

And in the power of that resurrection, those who put their faith in Jesus truly are given a new form of spiritual life in a way no mere secularized following His example can provide. By the example of His Sonship-death, we truly are imbued with a resurrection-power—yes, a fully miraculous, heavenly, spiritual power, the power of God Himself inside the hearts of all who invite His Spirit to live within them—to pray the

Sonship prayer of relinquishment ourselves: *Not my will, but Yours, God my Father.*

No magic makes this possible. His Sonship makes this possible, and with His Spirit's prompting and helping us from within, we have to follow in our own self-crucifying relinquishment.

His death and resurrection make it possible for His Spirit now to dwell within us, and for us to lay down our wills, and die into the will of the Father, as He did.

Perhaps this is my own way of saying with Lewis, "It works."

Which of the two views—belief or example—constitute "salvation"? Probably both.

Which is most important?

Again, probably both. Only God knows how they balance and harmonize in daily life, and what will be the precise parameters of the salvation equation that He will use for each individual.

Our salvation was not won by some act of celestial magic, but in the obedient Sonship of our Lord Jesus Christ.

His is an example we must make our own—in belief *and* lifestyle, in word *and* deed, by spirituality *and* obedience, loving God *and* man—if we are to enter into that salvation He won for us.

He modeled for us confession, baptism, goodness, death to self, kindness, sonship, trust in God, good deeds, love...dare we pick and choose from among these which we will follow, which are most important, and which comprise salvation?

We are not just called to be good secular people, we are called to be *Christlike* people, spiritual beings, citizens of a different Kingdom. We are called to walk with Christlike goodness, one with our Father in the midst of a secular and sinful world.

Sons and daughters.

Such is the life to which we are called.

We have to "die" with Christ, that we might be raised with Him to life eternal. We each have to discover the reality of that Sonship-death with Him.

No formula can nail the hands of the self to the cross.

We each must act as our own executioner.

PART 4

Life in Christ

Thirty-two

The Ultimate Creative Act

I WOULD LIKE TO PASS ON A TRUTH THAT HAS BEEN WONDERFULLY ILLUMI-
NATING AND HELPFUL TO ME as I have learned and experienced more
through the years of "dying with Christ." It comes from my spiritual and
literary mentor George MacDonald (1824-1905), 19th-century pastor, the-
ologian, and novelist.

To approach this truth, I would ask you to consider for a moment a
question: What is the grandest, most glorious thing that can be done in
this life?

What is the highest achievement possible?

What is the ultimate that this life has to offer any man or woman?

In answer, MacDonald speaks of a second "creation," brought to us,
exampled to us, and whose power is made available to us, by the Son of
God, Jesus Christ Himself.

The first creation, given the world by the Father, was fulfilled in the
first Adam. He was made in the image of God. As life was breathed into
Adam's nostrils, that first creation reached its crowning zenith. Life, *God's
own life*, was born within him.

What made the form of life given to Adam's race so unique? The gift
of a free and independent *will* that God placed into Him.

This WILL is the deepest, strongest, most God-like thing in man. It is
our link with God Himself, the piece of Himself He placed within us when
He created us "in His image."

We speak of the soul. But what is the most fundamental part of that
soul? What separates it from lower creature-life?

145

Not merely the ability to think. For though we obviously think on a far higher level, animals after their fashion can think as well. The distinction is the capacity to make moral decisions, to order our way according to right and wrong. It is what gives us a *spiritual* consciousness, and the potential to become spiritual beings. Free will.

Try to imagine the enormity of what God did—create beings that were *like* Him, and yet at the same time *separate* from Him. So separate, in fact, as to be capable of *choosing* or *not choosing* to have anything to do with Him.

What an astounding thing!

This fully free will we have been given is simply and unarguably the most remarkable aspect of the entire creation!

It is the only thing that is truly ours, *completely* ours, our very, very own. For having given it to us, God stepped back and in a sense bound the hands of His own omnipotence from interfering with it.

The wonder of the thing is beyond words!

God so honors the free will of man that He allows him to sink or swim with it...on his own.

In a sense, then, all of life, the foundational drama of existence, is nothing more than a living out of the question: What will we do with this magnificent possession with which God has endowed us?

How will we use the gift? What will we make of it?

This WILL is the *only* thing I really possess—that any of us have—that is truly mine. What will I do with it? It is the great story of life, of history, of eternity.

What will I—me, Michael Phillips, now, today!—do with *my* free will?

Naturally comes again the question, in a slightly different form, that I posed earlier: What is the *highest* thing I can do with it?

What is the *ultimate* use I can make of my WILL?

If I make the discovery of some wonderful place, what first comes to my mind?

To share it. To *give* the discovery to another.

If I make the acquaintance of a great book or a new author who excites me, as I have, in fact, during recent months, what is the first thing that comes to my mind? To share that discovery and knowledge...to *give* it to others.

Why did I want to give away my discovery of George MacDonald more than 30 years ago by editing and republishing his books? It was the highest and most wonderful use I could make of my discovery—to *give* it away.

The highest is always to *give*.

And is not the giving of what is *most* prized the best gift of all?

Many have called my work with MacDonald a "labor of love." And though I have been enriched abundantly by the process myself, and though it has only in very minor ways represented a "sacrifice," on another level that statement is not so far from the truth. Indeed, for many of the facsimiles we publish, we must break apart prized valuable editions in order to reprint them. These rare old original copies truly do "give their lives" that the truths within their pages may be available to many more.

The highest, then, is always to *give*. It is the reason why the most far-reaching love involves sacrifice, for to *give* most deeply always means one must give *oneself*.

"For God so loved the world that He gave..."

To *give*, to *yield*, to *give away*, even to *give up*...these are the ingredients of the highest forms of love we know how to express.

We come back, then, to the will. Not just any "will," an abstract will... but *your* will...and *my* will.

What is the highest, the deepest, the ultimate thing we can each do with our will?

I would pose this answer to that high question:

Yield it...abandon it...sacrifice it...and give it back to our Creator and Father who gave it to us in the first place.

We now approach holy ground, the pinnacle of what human life can and should and was intended to mean. When I asked in the previous chapter if you were willing to boldly venture up the hill of Calvary, there to discover childship, we at last now reach the apex of that climb.

The WILL is all we possess. To place it *back* into the hands of the Father, yielding it forever, represents the greatest—indeed the *perfect*—expression of human freedom. When Jesus commanded us, "Be perfect..."

I believe it was of this he was speaking—the laying down of the right to self-rule.

Such a self-willed abandonment is the greatest thing that can be accomplished in this life. In such an act do we reach the crowning apex of human personhood, the very culmination of what we were created to be.

Having achieved independence, adulthood, mature manhood and womanhood... to give up our right to them, to lay them down for the *greater* privilege of becoming children again—this is the greatest expression of personhood. Exactly as Jesus did—*I do nothing but what my Father tells me.*

We cannot become sons and daughters of childship any other way. This is where our childship is born, in our wills, and in laying these wills on the altar—an altar that is nothing more than the outspread loving hands of the Father who gave us our wills in the first place.

And when we place them into His hands, He gives personhood back to us, enriched, infused and filled with *His* life now in place of the meager self we gave up, a personhood of growing Christlikeness.

It is what Jesus came to teach us and show us how to do. In Him is this possibility born in us. In Him does such relinquished life come to flower. In Him are we made alive to God, His Father and ours. It is this new life, created by the Lord's obedience, that we are called to share in with Him.

No other creature can do this glorious thing. Only to man has been given this enormous potentiality—to lay down the very nature of humanity, and take God's nature instead.

This is what MacDonald calls "the creation in Christ," which comes to triumphant climax in the garden of Gethsemane, and then culminates the next day on the cross where, in relinquished Sonship, the salvation of the world was born.

Though "created" by Jesus, we must enter into this abandonment-life ourselves. He cannot do it for us. He has birthed the possibility. But only in the laying down of our own will, with His Spirit at work within us, do we bring such life alive within ourselves.

When we say, "Not my will but Yours be done," when we will the will of God and then do that will, then do we become one with God—a true son or daughter of our true Father.

148

Thirty-three

Living in Childship

IN RECOGNIZING THE REALITY OF OUR LORD'S HUMANITY, I would not be misunderstood as saying that we are more like Him, or He more like us, than I intend.

Truly He is like us in every respect...but one.

He faced all the struggles and temptations of the human free will...but He did not sin. We are and will forever remain part of fallen humanity. He is not. He was with God before the foundation of the world. He is God's Son because His being proceeds out of the very Godhead itself.

How a man could live as a mortal human and not sin is beyond our comprehension. That is what makes Him the Son of God, while we remain fallen sons and daughters of Adam. It is what makes Him our Savior.

In the living out of our childship according to His example and in the power of His resurrection, therefore, we recognize that we must do so in the midst of a fallen and sinful nature. A nature that *continues* to be fallen and sinful despite our most determined commitment and rigorous efforts to be God's children. A nature that continues to be fallen despite all the prayers we pray, despite invitations to God's Spirit to dwell within us and transform us, despite a strong and genuine desire to live as He would have us

Living in childship, therefore, will never be easy. Indeed, the moment childship becomes one's prayer, life becomes far *more* difficult until habits and patterns of self-rule are undone.

Swimming downstream in the world's flow is easy. You don't feel the strength of the current until you turn around and try to swim against it.

But the moment you tell your self that it is no longer to have its way, you are in for a fight!

Everything within us clamors for independence, for self-rule, for exaltation of self, for preeminence of *me* before you, for asking no other what I can or cannot do.

"No one is going to tell me what to do!" is the cry of our age. Christians think this way just like everyone else. Such a false priority is endemic to our culture. It is in the very air we breathe.

Never will your free will be so active and stir up such a ruckus as when you tell it, "Self, you must take the back seat now...you no longer dictate what I will do or think...self, you have no vote in my affairs...henceforth I take my instructions from Jesus Christ and Him only."

And believe me, once you take that stand against a soul and a self and a will that have been trained all their lives to demand and get their own way, the real work of discipleship sets in.

The angels may proclaim the hallelujahs of Christ's birth and rejoice in Heaven at the salvation of the lost sinner. God's people, on the other hand, are given the *hard work* of obedience and the yet *harder* work of putting the motives of an active self to death. It is a higher calling than that of the angels. For we must choose that obedience in the midst of fallen natures and weak wills.

We are no more angels than Jesus was. We are men and women. We have been given the highest privilege of creation—the laying down of self-will. We have been given the opportunity to share in the creation in Christ, to death ourselves into the will of God. It is a privilege no angel will ever know. Jesus Himself never uttered a recorded hallelujah. His praise was perfected in the words, *Not My will, but Yours be done.*

So, too, our obedience must be perfected in doing as He said. The life of the disciple is to fall on the knees in the solitude of childship and say, "What, Father, would You have me to do? You are my Father, I am Your obedient child. Speak, and I will obey. My only will is to do Your will."

And then get up and do it.

We must choose obedience in the midst of natures that would rather seek emotion and fellowship and activity and happiness and fun than the lonely discipleship of self-crucifying obedience. To the angels has been given the joy of lifting the hands in worship. Mankind is meant to learn obedience on its knees.

How, then, do we obey according to such childship? Of what is such obedience comprised?

Of nothing more or less than doing what Jesus said.

A thousand times, ten thousand times a year—how many times a day!—will the self rear its head in opposition to the practicality of His commands, screaming objections and whispering subtle justifications against the level of self-denial required?

Have I truly answered the final of the three crossroads questions? Am I willing to die with Him?

I honestly don't know.

Perhaps we can never know our own hearts well enough to answer that probing question. There is more than a little of Peter in us all. Words of commitment come easily. Deeds of self-denying death to self-motive are more difficult.

In one sense, I face the third crossroad every day of my life. Discipleship makes of the cross a moment by moment way of life, not an *end* to life. For most of us, dying with Him describes how we are to *live*, not a physical death we are likely to suffer.

Giving one's life in a glorious moment of sacrifice may even be easier; who can tell. But obeying the commands of Christ over a lifetime of 50 years, with all the thousand moments of sacrifice required, may be more demanding to the crucifying of the flesh than martyrdom.

Life with Him is *death* to self.

Every day leap to the forefront of my consciousness, clamoring for me to exalt and put my own priorities first, a hundred thoughts prompted by self, a dozen false priorities, a dozen petty frustrations, a dozen anxieties, a dozen selfishnesses, a dozen annoyances, a dozen worries, a dozen criticisms, a dozen attitudes and values that sneak into my brain and heart from the world.

"Quiet!" I must say, "I serve a different Master. Self, you do not rule. You dictate nothing of my affairs. Away with you. I will not listen to your arguments and rationalizations, your cunning lies. Begone, self, you do not rule here!"

It is laying aside my desire for independence, which is nothing more than *sin*-dependence, to link myself in every way with the Father's will for me instead of my own. It is hundreds of tiny deaths of self-relinquishment, over and over, day after day, year after year…

To lay down every ambition…hopes and dreams cherished in many areas of life, some large, some small…

To quell the onslaught of attitudes that bombard, trying to make me think in the world's way and according to its values…

To still worry, fretting, haste, frustration, disappointment, irritation…

To pray for those who wrong me, to go down on my knees and ask forgiveness for those I have wronged…and then get up from my knees and go to them and ask their forgiveness too…

To vanquish melancholy, impatience, rudeness, judgment, discouragement, complaint…

To see others as God sees them…to love them as He loves them…to give to them of myself as Jesus would were He at my side…

To trust God that all is well in the face of heartbreak…

Indeed, the self is a despot of a petty kingdom, an ousted monarch jealous to retake his throne at the slightest lapse of my defenses, at the least sign that I have ceased to guard one tiny flank against the intrusion of some unChristlike motive or attitude. The self is a cunning and willful part of my nature whose eye will forever lust after its former home, the throne of my WILL.

The lordship of Jesus Christ, and our childship as sons and daughters of His Father, is a self-chosen enslavement that must be reaffirmed in battle against this self daily, hourly, minute by minute.

Is it easy?

Relinquishing my own will is the hardest thing I ever do. If it is getting easier—and I am not quite sure—it is no less agonizing to the self now than when I began.

The way up Calvary carrying my own cross is a lifetime road. And the burden of relinquishment bites deep into the skin.

Thirty-four

The Commands

W<small>HY IS</small> J<small>ESUS AN OBEDIENT</small> S<small>ON</small>? B<small>ECAUSE</small> H<small>E DID THE WILL OF</small> H<small>IS</small> F<small>ATHER</small>.

Why did He come to earth? To show us how to do likewise, to subserve our wills, our priorities, our attitudes, our motives—to lay down self-rule itself—into the will of the Father.

In brief: He came to show us how to become obedient sons and daughters of God.

How do we learn this?

By following His example and doing the will of the Father like He did.

To take the guesswork out of it, Jesus gave us very specific instructions detailing exactly how we are to do so. Then He said, *"Keep these commands. Do what I have told you. This is how you show your love for Me. This is how the world will know that I came from the Father. Everything depends on whether you keep My commands."*

We have a very clear road map, then, into this obedient relationship with the Father He exampled for us. The doorway into our childship is nothing more or less than doing what Jesus said, following His Sonship into our own.

In obedience will our childship, like His, be born.

Not in church, not in fancy theology, not in the mass, not in worship, not in right doctrine, not in music, not in religious ritual, not in the rosary,

153

not in studying the Bible, not in what is commonly called ministry, not in formula, not in great works for God, not in a salvation prayer.

Only in *obedience* is childship born.

Those calling themselves Christians assume they understand the specific components of that obedience. Among them, it is probably fair to say that evangelicals flatter themselves that they understand it most clearly of all.

Such a one was I for many years. But in fact, though Jesus was in truth my Savior, and even my Lord, I understood very little of what His life signified. Though I was His follower, and had given my life to His service, His claim of obedience had not yet fully seized me. I did not know it, of course. Such inadequacies of shortsighted faith are usually revealed only in retrospect.

Then came a crisis in my spiritual pilgrimage when circumstances forced me to open the New Testament in a new way.

In the midst of this period of personal upheaval, my dear friend and pastor, with whom I had spent many hours in discussion over a period of years, said something during a vigorous exchange that struck root in my brain.

He challenged me to go to the Source for the answer to the quandary that was plaguing me at that moment.

"Find out what the Bible says," were the words of his simple ultimatum.

At first my reaction, I am sorry to admit, was probably laced with a certain degree of pride.

"Who...me? I already know what the Bible says."

And in fact, my line of defense wasn't so far wrong. Indeed I had studied the Bible for years. I had read it cover to cover. Most pages of my favorite brown leather Bible contained underlinings and markings. I considered that I knew my New Testament just about inside out. I had taught classes on apologetics, on the Books of Mark and John, and would have said I knew the Gospels inside out.

But somehow the challenge he threw down that day rang new in my ear. He made his statement thinking to convince me of his point of view in a certain matter that had become a sticking point between us. As we are all prone to do, he assumed that my study of the biblical texts would confirm *his* position. We all use the Bible, and I am surely no exception, to confirm our *own* positions—resulting in diametrically opposite doctrinal positions *both* being validated from Scripture. We read into the Bible what we want to read into it.

However, in this case my pastor's words took on a much wider import and scope. I realized I needed to find out what the Bible said, not about this one issue, but about everything!

What was the New Testament imperative upon my life?

Not in some grandiose, far-reaching way…but close beside me. Where I lived. In the next five minutes.

If I had to summarize in a few words what being a Christian meant to me, what would I say? What was the *essence*, the foundation of spirituality?

Boiled down. The raw guts of the gospel. No frills. No excess baggage. No trite little phrases I had learned in Sunday school or youth group or that I had written down from a sermon…or even that I had taught others as I stood at the lectern myself.

No pat phrases like, *Live for God*, or, *Serve the Lord*, or *Believe in Jesus as my personal Lord and Savior*, or *Trust in the Holy Spirit*, or *Fellowship with the Body of Christ*, or *Just give it to God*.

A year before I might have been spouting such phrases to describe my life too. But they were no good to me now. No longer could I find practicality in them. They didn't *say* anything.

I needed an anchor that could give validity to an entire life's purpose and perspective as a Christian…and at the same time that could explain how I was to live and behave in the next five minutes, no matter what life threw at me.

I needed to find the link between *belief* and *practice*; between *eternity* and *now*; between Christianity as a world religion, and Christianity as a practical guidebook for going about the business of life in the trenches.

Those pat phrases of learned religiosity couldn't do that.

Perhaps, I thought, the solution to my conundrum lay in the Gospels themselves. In the very Book I had been teaching with such enthusiasm, Mark, as well as the accounts of his three colleagues. For if ever a man walked in harmony between *ultimate purpose* and *the next five minutes*, that man was Jesus Christ.

Might I be able to discover the spiritual essentiality I sought there...in His life? Was that where the mysterious link between eternity and now was meant to be unlocked...where one could discover what has been called the eternal now?

But it wouldn't do just to read the story again as I had already read it and studied it and taught it dozens of times.

I knew I had to go back to the Book, as if for the first time, and read it afresh.

As I challenged you at the beginning, I had to find a way to get inside the account myself. I had to put myself into the story.

And so when I took my pastor and friend up on his challenge, and carved out a time in my schedule to go away and seclude myself for a week, I took with me no book other than my Bible.

Even that I did not take to study, as I had always studied. It was a far simpler assignment I set for myself.

It was nothing more or less than to find out what Jesus said. Not as read in a book, but as heard by an eyewitness...me!

When I opened my Bible and began to read anew, I did so as someone looking for what I had been told to do.

No commentaries, no books, no concordances, no inductive Bible studies, no notebooks cluttered my table as I began to immerse myself in the astonishing tale told by Matthew, Mark, Luke, and John.

Only the account itself of that life. Just the words on the page. Nothing else. I chose a Bible for the occasion that contained no footnotes or cross references. If the raw dynamic of that life truly had power to change the world, I now had to find out if it had the power to change *me*.

So I put myself into the story...hearing it...feeling it...thinking of myself now as one of the 12, now as one of the 70, now as one of the multitude...watching, observing, following, listening.

Listening to the words of Jesus.

Listening as He instructed, as He exhorted, as He taught, as He encouraged, as He commanded...listening to what He said about God, listening to what He said about Himself, listening to the specifics He told His disciples and followers to obey.

To get a handle on these specifics, I began reading at Matthew 1:1 and listed *every* specific command or directive given to the Lord's disciples, and every quality emphasized as a required element of character in the life of the disciple.

It turned out to be a bigger project than I had anticipated. Hoping to find the answer to one ambiguous doctrinal issue, I realized I was onto something powerful. Beyond all the doctrine and theology of the Bible, just what exactly had we been commanded to *do*?

It was the most eye-opening study I have ever done. I have the papers beside me at this moment more than 25 years later. As I peruse them again I am struck with the simplicity yet eternal enormity of Jesus' down-to-earth commands and instructions.

When I was through, I loosely grouped and categorized similar commands to make the list manageable. The results may surprise you, as they did me. But no longer was there any doubt in my mind about just what Jesus meant when He said, "If you love Me you will keep My commandments."

Now I knew exactly what those commands were. They were in front of me in black and white.

They left my SELF, my WILL, my SOUL, my FLESH, my INDEPENDENCE, no place to hide. They were so practical and down-to-earth, no longer could my discipleship be a vague matter of belief and worship and church involvement and ministry.

It was as near as my neighbor. Suddenly here was Jesus speaking to *me*. I had been drawn into the dramatic story myself. And these were His commands...to *me*.

Many such issues rose within me during that week spent with the Gospels.

In their pages I found no magician. I found obedient Sonship.

This is neither the time nor the place to attempt a detailed study of the list I compiled. I simply present to you the information as I discovered it and as I categorized the commands of Jesus. I suppose in a way it speaks for itself. You may take it and use it in your life as you feel God would have you.

No doubt I missed some commands that a more careful scrutiny would uncover. Mine was intended as a devotional study, not a computer-perfect one. I have gone to my knees more than once since then and during this present writing, asking God to deepen my sonship yet more. I am not trying to satisfy *intellects* with a perfect list as exhaustive as Strong's Concordance. I pray rather that this stirs *hearts* to seek the spirit of Christ and His desire for our lives.

My categorizations may not be to your liking. Included are both direct and indirect commands, some of which Jesus emphasizes as attitudes and qualities of character important in the life of the disciple. Clearly I had to combine as many as possible. Thus, a command such as, "Be perfect," along with the implied quality inherent in a statement such as, "Unless your righteousness exceeds that of the Pharisees," are both included in the grouping to which I gave the label, *Be righteous.*

I have set down most of what Jesus said to His disciples, but not the commands to others or, as in the parables, statements that seem to have little universal or direct bearing on you and me today.

For example, when Jesus says, "Watch out for the leaven of the Pharisees," I felt that to be a command with a certain universal application, and therefore included it in the category of commands, *Be careful, watchful, alert, on guard.* But when He said, "Pick up your mat and go home," I felt that this did not contain the same kind of direct application (though some may disagree) and therefore did not include it in my list.

When, on the other hand, Jesus said, as He did frequently, "Listen..." to introduce some specific teaching, feeling that it was a command of some significance, I included it among those others exhorting us to, *Listen, listen carefully,* etc.

What follow are listed in approximate order of frequency mentioned—the first two, for example, appear twenty-six times each, *Don't worry* eight times, *Forgive* four times, and the entire last half only once or twice. (See also Appendix Three.)

With these words—so familiar, yet newly powerful—in our ears, I shrink from attempting a rousing dramatic conclusion to this time we have spent together thinking and praying about the obedient Sonship of Jesus. I would not have my words add or subtract from His.

Therefore, let us allow the commands of Jesus to speak for themselves. Jesus said:

> *Be careful, watchful, alert, on guard...Take heart, take courage, don't be afraid...Listen, listen carefully; be clear-minded; apply yourself to think, learn, and understand.*
>
> *Love, love God, love man...Do good toward and pray for your adversaries...Follow Me...Pray...Give when asked; give and do more than required...Care for the oppressed, give to the poor...Don't worry...Deny yourself, lose your life...Believe.*
>
> *Be at peace, reconciled, and united with others...If part of your body sins, get rid of it...Do good...Let children come to Me...Proclaim the Kingdom of God...Do good, pray, and fast unseen by others...Be a servant...Forgive...Forgive 70 x 7 times...Obey My commands... Obey the commandments...Give to the government what belongs to it, and to God what belongs to Him...Seek first God's Kingdom; store up treasure in Heaven.*
>
> *Do not exalt yourself...Trust and have faith in God...Be righteous...Do not be called teacher...Don't separate what God has joined...Abide in Me... Worship the Lord and serve Him only.*
>
> *Do to others as you would have them do to you...Don't judge...Deal with your own faults before the faults of others...Rejoice...Ask...Seek...Knock...Enter through the narrow gate...Make disciples of all nations...Bring Me your burdens...Take My yoke on you.*
>
> *Give up everything...Be glad...Don't swear...Say what you mean...Don't resist evil people...Teach people to obey what I have commanded...Have salt in yourselves...Repent.*
>
> *Show mercy...Don't condemn...Don't take the place of honor...Don't judge by appearances...Wash each other's feet...Don't doubt...Be shrewd as snakes, innocent as doves...Obey the Word of God.*

The stirring I feel in my own heart at this moment is simply to quietly pray,

"Lord Jesus, help me to do as You have commanded me."

With this list before us, then, I know of no more fitting way to close, than simply to prayerfully remind ourselves of the Lord's words:

> *Whoever has My commands and obeys them, he is the one who loves Me...If anyone loves Me, he will obey My teaching (John 14:21a,23a, NIV).*

> *If you love Me, you will obey what I command (John 14:15, NIV).*

In obedience was His Sonship perfected. In obedience will our childship grow.

Appendices

Appendix One

The Creation in Christ

Excerpts from "The Creation in Christ" by George MacDonald,
Unspoken Sermons, Third Series, 1889
(Reprinted in *Discovering the Character of God*, 1990)

When a man can and does entirely say, "Not my will, but thine be done," when he so wills the will of God as to do it, then is he one with God—one, as a true son with a true Father. When a man wills that his being be conformed to the being of his origin, which is the life of his life...when the man thus accepts his own causing life, *and sets himself to live the will of that causing life*, humbly eager after the privileges of his origin, thus receiving God, he becomes, in the act, a partaker of the divine nature, a true son of the living God, and an heir of all he possesses.

By the obedience of a son, he receives into himself the very life of the Father.

Men speak of the so-called *creations* of the human intellect or of the human imagination. But there is nothing man can do that comes half so near the true "making," the true creativity of the Maker as the ordering of his own way. There is only one thing that is higher, the highest creation of which man is capable, and that is to will the will of the Father. That act indeed contains within it an element of the purely creative, and when man does will such, then he is most like God.

To do what we ought, as children of God, is an altogether higher, more divine, more potent, more creative thing, than to write the grandest poem, paint the most beautiful picture, carve the mightiest statue, build the most magnificent temple, dream out the most enchanting symphony…

By actively willing the will of God and doing what of it lies within his power, the man takes the share offered him in his own making, in his own becoming. In willing actively and operatively to become what he was made to be, he becomes creative—so far as a man may. In this way also he becomes like his Father in heaven…

Obedience is the joining of the links of the eternal round. Obedience is but the other side of the creative will. Will is God's will; obedience is man's will; the two make one.

Man cannot originate this life. It must be shown him, and he must choose it. God is the Father of Jesus and of us—of every possibility of our being. But while God is the Father of his children, Jesus is the father of their sonship, for in Him is made the life which is sonship to the Father—the recognition, in fact and life, that the Father has his claim upon his sons and daughters.

We are not and cannot become true sons and daughters without our will willing his will, our doing following his making. It was the will of Jesus to be the thing God willed and meant him, that made him the true Son of God. He was not the Son of God because he could not help it, but because he willed to be in himself the Son that he was in the divine idea.

So with us: we must *be* the sons we are. We must be sons and daughters in our will. And we can be sons and daughters, saved into the bliss of our being, only by choosing God for the Father he is, and doing his will—yielding ourselves true sons and daughters to the absolute Father…

The love of the Son is responsive to the love of the Father. The response to self-existent love is self-abnegating love. The refusal of himself is that in Jesus which corresponds to the creation of God.

His love takes action, it *creates*, in self-abjuration, in the death of self as motive. *That* is the moment of highest creation—in the willing laying down of self into the Father's will, in the drowning of self in the life of God, where it lives only as love.

In that willing yielding of his self is *life* created. Such is the life spoken of by the Apostle John when he said, "That which was made in him was life."

And truly, that life is the light of men!…

164

The life of Christ is this—that he does nothing, cares for nothing for his own sake, because he cares with his whole soul for the will, the pleasure of his Father. Because his Father is his Father, therefore he will be his child. The truth in Jesus is his relation to his Father; the righteousness of Jesus is his fulfillment of that relation.

Loving his Father thus with his whole being, Jesus is not merely alive as born of God, but, giving himself with perfect will to God, choosing to die to himself and live to God, he therein creates in himself a new and higher life. And standing upon himself, he has gained the power to awaken life, the divine shadow of his own, in the hearts of his brothers and sisters, who have come from the same birth-home as himself, namely, the heart of his God and our God, his Father and our Father. To will, not from self, but with the Eternal, is to live.

The choice of his own being, in the full knowledge of what he did— this active willing to be the Son of the Father, perfect in obedience—is that in Jesus which responds and corresponds to the self-existence of God. Jesus rose at once to the height of his being, set himself down on the throne of his nature, in the act of subjecting himself to the will of the Father as his only good, the only *reason* for his existence. When he died on the cross, he did, in the wild weather of his outlying provinces, in the torture of the body of his revelation, that which he had done at home in glory and gladness. From the infinite beginning—for here I can speak only by contradictions—he completed and held fast the eternal circle of his existence in saying, "Thy will, not mine, be done!" He made himself what he is by *deathing* himself into the will of the eternal Father, through which he was the eternal Son—thus plunging into the fountain of his own life, the everlasting Fatherhood, and taking the Godhead of the Son.

This is the life that was made *in* Jesus: "That which was made in him was life."

This life, self-willed in Jesus, is the one thing that makes such life the eternal life, the true life, possible—no, imperative, essential, to every man, woman, and child, whom the Father has sent into the outer, that they may go back into the inner world, his heart. As the self-existent life of the Father has given us being, so the willed devotion of Jesus is his power to give us eternal life like his own—to enable us to do the same. There is no life for any one, other than the same kind that Jesus has; Jesus' disciple must live by the same absolute devotion of his will to the Father's. Then is the disciple's life one with the life of the Father...

The bond of the universe, the chain that holds it together, the one active unity, the harmony of things, the negation of difference, the reconciliation of all forms and all wandering desires, the fact at the root of every vision, is the devotion of the Son to the Father. It is the life of the universe...

We can live in no way but that in which Jesus lived, in which life was made in him. That way is to give up our life. This is the one supreme action of life possible to us for the making of life in ourselves.

Christ did it of himself, and so became light to us, that we might be able to do it in ourselves, after him, through his originating act. But we must do it ourselves. The help that he has given and gives us every moment, the light and the spirit-working of the Lord, the Spirit, in our hearts, is all there that we may, as we must, do it ourselves. Until then we are not alive; life is not made in us.

The whole strife and labor and agony of the Son with every man is to get him to die as he died...

If I say not with my whole heart, "My father, do with me as thou wilt, only help me against myself and for thee"; if I cannot say, "I am thy child, the inheritor of thy Spirit, let me be thine in any shape the love that is my Father may please to have me"; if we cannot, fully as this, give ourselves to the Father, then we have not yet laid hold upon that for which Christ has laid hold upon us.

When a man or woman truly and perfectly says with Jesus, and as Jesus said it, "Thy will be done," he closes the everlasting life-circle. The life of the Father and the Son flows through him; he is a part of the divine organism. Then is the prayer of the Lord in him fulfilled: "I in them and thou in me, that they may be made perfect in one." The Christ in us is the Spirit of the perfect child toward the perfect Father. The Christ in us is our own true nature made to blossom in us by the Lord, whose life is the light of men that it may become the life of men; for our true nature is childhood to the Father.

Appendix Two

Self-denial

Excerpts from "Self Denial" by George MacDonald,
Unspoken Sermons, Second Series, 1885
(Reprinted in *Knowing the Heart of God,* 1990)

We must become as little children, and Christ must be born in us; we must learn of him, and the one lesson he has to give is himself: he does first all he wants us to do; he is first all he wants us to be. We must not merely do as he did; we must see things as he saw them, regard them as he regarded them; we must take the will of God as the very life of our being; we must neither try to get our own way, nor trouble ourselves as to what may be thought or said of us. The world must be to us as nothing.

By the world I mean all ways of judging, regarding, and thinking, whether political, economical, ecclesiastical, social, or individual, which are not...God's ways of thinking, regarding, or which do not take God into account, do not set his will supreme...From everything that is against the teaching and thinking of Jesus, from the world in the heart of the best man in it, specially from the world in his own heart, the disciple must turn to follow him...To follow him is to leave one's self behind, "If any man would come after me, let him deny himself."...

Verily it is not to thwart or tease the poor self Jesus tells us. That was not the purpose for which God gave it to us! He tells us we must leave it altogether—yield it, deny it, refuse it, lose it: thus only shall we save it, thus only have a share in our own being. The self is given to us that we may sacrifice it; it is ours that we like Christ may have somewhat to offer—not that we should torment it, but that we should deny it; not that we should cross it, but that we should abandon it utterly...

"What can this mean?—we are not to thwart, but to abandon? How abandon, without thwarting?"

It means this:—we must refuse, abandon, deny self altogether as a ruling, or determining, or originating element in us. It is to be no longer the regent of our action. We are no more to think, "What should I like to do?" but "What would the Living One have me do?"...The Self is God's making—only it must be the 'slave of Christ,' that the Son may make it also the free son of the same Father...

The time will come when it shall be so possessed, so enlarged, so idealized, by the indwelling God, who is its deeper, its deepest self, that there will be no longer any enforced denial of it needful: it has been finally denied and refused and sent into its own obedient place; it has learned to receive with thankfulness, to demand nothing; to turn no more upon its own centre, or any more think to minister to its own good. God's eternal denial of himself, revealed in him who for our sakes in the flesh took up his cross daily, will have been developed in the man; his eternal rejoicing will be in God—and in his fellows...

To deny oneself then, is to act no more from the standing-ground of self; to allow no private communication, no passing influence between the self and the will; not to let the right hand know what the left hand doeth. No grasping or seeking, no hungering of the individual, shall give motion to the will; no desire to be conscious of worthiness shall order the life; no ambition whatever shall be a motive of action; no wish to surpass another be allowed a moment's respite from death; no longing after the praise of men influence a single throb of the heart...

Right deeds, and not the judgment thereupon; true words, and not what reception they may have, shall be our care. Not merely shall we not love money, or trust in it, or seek it as the business of life, but, whether we have it or have it not, we must never think of it as a windfall from the tree of event or the cloud of circumstance, but as the gift of God.

We must draw our life, by the uplooking, acknowledging will, every moment fresh from the living one, the causing life, not glory in the mere consciousness of health and being. It is God [who] feeds us, warms us, quenches our thirst.

The will of God must be to us all in all; to our whole nature the life of the Father must be the joy of the child; we must know our very understanding his—that we live and feed on him every hour in the closest, veriest way: to know these things in the depth of our knowing, is to deny ourselves, and take God instead...

So must we deny all anxieties and fears. When young we must not mind what the world calls failure; as we grow old, we must not be vexed that we cannot remember, must not regret that we cannot do, must not be miserable because we grow weak or ill: we must not mind anything. We have to with God who can, not with ourselves where we cannot; we have to do with the Will, with the Eternal Life of the Father of our spirits, and not with the being which we could not make, and which is his care. He is our care; we are his; our care is to will his will; his care, to give us all things. This is to deny ourselves.

"Self, I have not to consult you, but him whose idea is the soul of you, and of which as yet you are all unworthy...You may be my consciousness, but you are not my being. If you were, what a poor, miserable, dingy, weak wretch I should be! but my life is hid with Christ in God, whence it came, and whither it is returning—with you certainly, but as an obedient servant, not a master. Submit, or I will cast you from me, and pray to have another consciousness given me. For God is more to me than my consciousness of myself. He is my life; you are only so much of it as my poor half-made being can grasp—as much of it as I can now know at once. Because I have fooled and spoiled you, treated you as if you were indeed my own self, you have dwindled yourself and have lessened me, till I am ashamed of myself...

"Good-bye, Self! I deny you, and will do my best every day to leave you behind me."...

When Jesus tells us we must follow him...he speaks first and always as *the Son* of the Father...He is the Son of the Father as the Son who obeys the Father, as the Son who came expressly and only to do the will of the

169

Father, as the messenger whose delight it is to do the will of him that sent him. At the moment he says *Follow me*, he is following the Father; his face is set homeward. He would have us follow him because he is bent on the will of the Blessed…. To believe in him is to do as he does, to follow him where he goes. We must believe in him practically—altogether practically, as he believed in his Father…

It is not to follow him to take him in any way theoretically, to hold this or that theory about why he died, or wherein lay his atonement: such things can be revealed only to those who follow him in his active being and the principle of his life—who do as he did, live as he lived. There is no other following. He is all for the Father; we must be all for the Father too, else are we not following him. To follow him is to be learning of him, to think his thoughts, to use his judgments, to see things as he saw them, to feel things as he felt them, to be hearted, souled, minded, as he was— that so also we may be of the same mind with his Father.

This it is to deny self and go after him; nothing less, even if it be working miracles and casting out devils, is to be his disciple. Busy from morning to night doing great things for him on any other road, we should but earn the reception, 'I never knew you.' When he says, 'Take my yoke upon you, '…The will of the Father is the yoke he would have us take, and bear also with him. It is of this yoke that he says, It is easy, of this burden, It is light…With the garden of Gethsemane before him, with the hour and the power of darkness waiting for him, he declares his yoke easy, his burden light. There is no magnifying of himself. He first denies himself, and takes up his cross—then tells us to do the same. The Father magnifies the Son, not the Son himself; the Son magnifies the Father.

We must be jealous for God against ourselves, and look well to the cunning and deceitful Self—ever cunning and deceitful until it is informed of God—until it is thoroughly and utterly denied…While it is not denied, only thwarted, we may through satisfaction with conquered difficulty and supposed victory, minister yet more to its self-gratulation…

In a thousand ways will Self delude itself, in a thousand ways befool its own slavish being. Christ sought not his own, sought not anything but the will of his Father: we have to grow diamond-clear, true as the white light of the morning. Hopeless task!—were it not that he offers to come himself, and dwell in us...

We must note that, although the idea of the denial of self is an entire and absolute one, yet the thing has to be done daily: we must keep on denying. It is a deeper and harder thing than any sole effort of most herculean will may finally effect. For indeed the will itself is not pure, is not free, until the Self is absolutely denied...

Is there not many a Christian who, having begun to deny himself, yet spends much strength in the vain and evil endeavour to accommodate matters between Christ and the dear Self—seeking to save that which so he must certainly lose—in how different a way from that in which the Master would have him lose it: It is one thing to have the loved self devoured of hell in hate and horror and disappointment; another to yield it to conscious possession by the living God himself, who will raise it then first and only to its true individuality, freedom, and life...

Here is the promise to those who will leave all and follow him : "Whosoever shall lose his life, for my sake, the same shall save it,"...

What speech of men or angels will serve to shadow the dimly glorious hope! To lose ourselves in the salvation of God's heart! to be no longer any care to ourselves, but know God taking divinest care of us, his own! to be and feel just a resting-place for the divine love...to know that God and we mean the same thing, that we are in the secret, the child's secret of existence, that we are pleasing in the eyes and to the heart of the Father! to live nestling at his knee, climbing to his bosom, blessed in the mere and simple being which is one with God, and is the outgoing of his will, justifying the being by the very facts of the being, by its awareness of itself as bliss! what a self is this to receive again from him for that we left, forsook, refused! We left it paltry, low, mean; he took up the poor cinder of a consciousness, carried it back to the workshop of his spirit, made it a true thing, radiant, clear, fit for eternal companying and indwelling, and restored it to our having and holding for ever!

Appendix Three

Commands Given

Commands Given to the Lord's Disciples	Number of Times in Gospels
Be careful, watchful, alert, on guard	26
Take heart, take courage, don't be afraid	26
Listen, listen carefully; be clear-minded; apply yourself to think, learn, and understand	18
Love, love God, love man	17
Do good toward and pray for your adversaries	13
Follow Me	13
Pray	12
Give when asked; give and do more than required	12
Care for the oppressed, give to the poor	9
Don't worry	8
Deny yourself, lose your life	8
Believe	7
Be at peace, reconciled, and united with other	6
If part of your body sins, get rid of it	6
Do good	5
Let children come to Me	5
Proclaim the Kingdom of God	5
Do good, pray, and fast unseen by others	4
Be a servant	4
Forgive	3
Forgive 70 x 7 times	1
Obey My command	4
Obey the commandments	3
Give to the government what belongs to it, and to God what belongs to Him	3

Commands Given to the Lord's Disciples	Number of Times in Gospels
Seek first God's Kingdom; store up treasure in Heaven	3
Do not exalt yourself	3
Trust and have faith in God	3
Be righteous	2
Do not be called teacher	2
Don't separate what God has joined	2
Abide in Me	2
Worship the Lord and serve Him only	2
Do to others as you would have them do to you	2
Don't judge	2
Deal with your own faults before the faults of others	2
Rejoice	2
Ask	2
Seek	2
Knock	2
Enter through the narrow gate	2
Make disciples of all nations	2
Bring Me your burdens	1
Take My yoke on you	1
Give up everything	1
Be glad	1
Don't swear	1
Say what you mean	1
Don't resist evil people	1
Teach people to obey what I have commanded	1
Have salt in yourselves	1
Repent	1
Show mercy	1
Don't condemn	1
Don't take the place of honor	1
Don't judge by appearances	1
Wash each other's feet	1
Don't doubt	1
Be shrewd as snakes, innocent as doves	1
Obey the word of God	1

Books by Michael Phillips

GOD: A GOOD FATHER

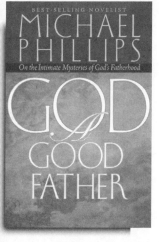

In this startling book, Michael Phillips challenges the established Christian to step out of the status quo and into a breathtaking new relationship with God the Father. In a style reminiscent of John Bunyan's classic *Pilgrim's Progress*, Phillips acts as a "guide" on a journey to the place of the presence of our Heavenly Father. A "divine restlessness" within you will be inspired as you follow Phillips out of the "fogbound lowlands" of your typical existence and climb to the "mountain home of Abba Father," learning to know Him—His love, His goodness, His trustworthiness, His forgiveness—and choosing to live in His heart and drink of His water of life forever!
ISBN: 0-7684-2123-3

DESTINY JUNCTION

Destiny Junction is a small town, not unlike any other small town in America. As its name implies, however, it becomes the place where many people's lives meet destiny. Through one young lady's obedient Christian life and the work of the Holy Spirit subsequent to her tragic death, the lives of many people in the town of Destiny Junction are transformed. This is their story...a story about life...and what it means...or what it ought to mean.
ISBN: 0-7684-2062-8

COMING IN THE WINTER OF 2002

KINGS CROSSROADS
ISBN: 0-7684-2152-7

Available at your local Christian bookstore.

Additional copies of this book and other
book titles from DESTINY IMAGE are
available at your local bookstore.

For a complete list of our titles,
visit us at www.destinyimage.com
Send a request for a catalog to:

Destiny Image® Publishers, Inc.
P.O. Box 310
Shippensburg, PA 17257-0310

*"Speaking to the Purposes of God for This
Generation and for the Generations to Come"*